The Bumper Book
of Government Waste

The scandal of the
squandered billions
from Lord Irvine's
wallpaper to EU saunas

by

Matthew Elliott
Lee Rotherham

Harriman House Ltd
43 Chapel Street
Petersfield
Hampshire
GU32 3DY

Tel: +44 (0)1730 233870
Fax: +44 (0)1730 233880
Email: enquiries@harriman-house.com
Website: www.harriman-house.com

First published in Great Britain in 2006 by Harriman House Ltd.
Copyright Harriman House Ltd

The rights of Matthew Elliott and Lee Rotherham to be identified
as the authors has been asserted in accordance with the
Copyright, Design and Patents Act 1988.

Cartoon illustrations by Ed McLachlan

ISBN 1-897-59779-7
ISBN13 978-1-897597-79-8

British Library Cataloguing in Publication Data
A CIP catalogue record for this book can be obtained from the
British Library

Printed and bound by Biddles.

About the authors

Matthew Elliott was born in Leeds and attended the local Grammar School, where he was taught French by Joanne Harris, the author of *Chocolat*. He moved to London in 1997 to study at the London School of Economics, where he had the double success of graduating with a First and meeting his future brother-in-law. After stints in a think tank, the House of Commons and the European Parliament, he founded the TaxPayers' Alliance in 2004 with Andrew Allum and Florence Heath. He is currently the TPA's Chief Executive and a well known commentator on government waste and the case for lower taxes.

Dr Lee Rotherham holds two research degrees on French Canada, a subject so esoteric it automatically makes him a world expert. He is also by background a linguist and historian. His Mediaeval Occitan was just one of several languages that proved to be absolutely useless when he acted as an adviser on the Convention that drafted the thoroughly despicable EU Constitution. He has also advised three successive Shadow Foreign Secretaries, though the turnover wasn't his fault. As a TA reservist, his introduction to government waste was when he got mobilized and spent time living in one of Saddam's palaces, where the loos didn't work. A prominent Eurosceptic, hunted across the continent by bands of pro-Brussels politicians carrying lit torches and pitchforks, he has been widely published.

Acknowledgements

The Bumper Book of Government Waste is built on two shorter Bumper Books published by the TaxPayers' Alliance in 2004 and 2005. Help with those publications and advice on this book came from TPA founders Andrew Allum and Florence Heath and campaign team members Mario Chacon-Pearse, James Frayne, Mitesh Karia, Saul Rowe and Eben Wilson.

We would like to thank MPs John Hayes and Mike Penning, and MEPs Chris Heaton-Harris and Jens-Peter Bonde, for their assistance with researching this book and for their tireless work in holding people who hold the purse strings to account. And TPA Research Officer Peter Cuthbertson for researching and drafting the section on public sector jobs.

Thanks also to David Wilkinson who assisted in our detailed costings of three new articulated lorries crammed with plastic ducks without asking any questions. Apart from, "The Diana Memorial costs £200k a year? What is it, a fountain or a hospital?"

Contents

Section Three: Other Areas of Waste

Section Four: Waste and Extravagance in Perspective

Conclusion

Appendices

Foreword

It is an axiomatic truth that people take better care of their own possessions than other people's. Just look at how carelessly employees drive company cars compared to their own. And when it comes to state assets, the ownership connection is very distant indeed. So the inevitable happens: people are not really that bothered when it comes to squandering government money.

Sadly, this money is real money – it belongs to taxpayers, who have worked hard to earn it. Through legalised theft, Parliament sequesters it to fritter on more or less anything it fancies. So for example, MPs have over the years voted through improvements to their Parliamentary Contributory Pension Fund, which make it one of the most generous final salary pension schemes of its kind anywhere in the world. Lucky them! But pretty tough for the rest of us, who have to fund their self-enrichment.

And these principles can be extended right across the public sector. While there are many conscientious staff in the state sector, generally governments are unwise custodians of property of almost any kind. Just look at how New Labour gave away QinetiQ to US buyout house Carlyle, due to make a nine-fold return in a few years. Ultimately for the state there is never the threat of bankruptcy, which acts as a spur to keep the private sector efficient. And there is no competition to squeeze out profligacy. So when politicians decide they need to spend more money, they just increase their rate of robbery – sorry tax – to pay for their ill-advised projects. They don't have to worry about a rival offering the same product or service at a lower price and driving them out of business. Free markets protect corporate abuse in the capitalist system – but governments are exempt from such rigour.

This book attempts to itemise the scandalous abuses suffered by taxpayers at the hands of our Political Masters. It shows how through department overspend, public sector fraud, quangos, the EU, government overmanning, over-generous state employee pensions, state IT projects, and hundreds of other ways, the government wastes as much as £82 billion of our money every year. This works out to almost £1,400 for every man, woman and child in the UK – perhaps 20 per cent of all state spending.

The authors have done a pretty thorough job in cataloguing a decent sample of the endless mismanagement and extravagance that characterises so much of central and local government. Many of the tales will anger you – some will make you laugh – and some should make you weep. The sums involved are occasionally relatively trifling – Ofsted's new office plants at £500 each, for example. Others are so large they beggar belief: central government administration now costs £21.3 billion a year – an increase of over 40 per cent since 1998, itself a period of low inflation.

The problem with taxation is two-fold: firstly governments seize your money and misuse it; then they subject you to a tax system which is a Byzantine mess, capable of tripping up even the most honest and diligent citizen. As Nobel Prize winner Albert

Einstein said: "The hardest thing in the world to understand is the income tax." The costs of administering the current tax regime are monstrous, and one of the huge benefits of a flat tax scheme would be to simplify the paperwork and reduce the bureaucracy.

Sadly few politicians and civil servants are ever willing to cut public spending. This means reducing their influence, which they hate to do. Moreover, through excessive government spending MPs create client voters, who come to rely on hand-outs of one form or another. Such welfare dependency is profoundly damaging to a civil society: it encourages bad behaviour and punishes hard work. There is now a profound mismatch in public spending between the highly productive South-East of England, and the North-East, North-West, Wales, Scotland and Northern Ireland. Curiously enough, voters in these latter regions seem keen on electing tax and spend politicians – while the South of England now has a lower share of government spending than any rich country except South Korea.

Unless there is serious reform in the public sector then our overall standard of living will fall relative to others. In a global economy we can no longer afford the perverse incentives and immorality of high taxes and unnecessary government spending. Competition across every industry means the private sector – which ultimately funds all tax payments – has to fight harder than ever to keep customers and jobs. Research has shown that if you shake up welfare spending, even the poorest will be better off. It requires serious effort and brave statesmen. This book is a useful primer to encourage those in power to do some hard thinking, and perhaps spark them into action. There is no time to be lost.

Luke Johnson
Chairman of Channel 4 Television
and Risk Capital Partners, a private equity firm.

Section One

Introduction to Government Waste

"I don't know whether Marx ever said waste is theft from the working class, but he should have."

Patricia Hewitt (Labour MP and cabinet minister)

Introduction

Welcome to the world of government waste. You are about to enter a twilight zone of crazy spending, political correctness, utter incompetence, and fantastic jollies used to throw taxpayers' money around like there's no tomorrow.

It's easy to forget that all this money has to come from somewhere, even if 'central government' or 'the council' is the one spending it. Be under no illusion: it comes from *you*.

In the pages that follow, we have highlighted a myriad, indeed a veritable plethora, of examples of government waste and useless spending, taken from thousands held on file. The figures have been compiled from official reports, media coverage and government statistics – none of which is entirely trustworthy, but which do at least provide a conservative measure of the amount of money going down the plughole. Full sources for each item can be found on the TaxPayers' Alliance website.*

---

* www.taxpayersalliance.com

Added together, the wasteful and useless spending comes to *£82 billion*. That's more than the annual turnover of nineteen European countries. Or more than £4,000 per family in Britain.

If you wasted your family's money on this scale, you would probably be locked up. So why does the Government think it can get away with it?

We define waste as everything from government extravagance, such as Lord Irvine's wallpaper, to overspending on government projects, such as the NHS National Programme for IT (NPfIT), which is fives times over budget and will deliver an outdated product if ever completed. It doesn't even play Minesweeper.

Waste also covers what we consider to be *useless* spending – money spent on schemes or initiatives that might do some good, but where the value added by the scheme falls well short of the cost to taxpayers. A classic example is the Department of Trade and Industry, which delivers output but is poor value for money.

Government waste is, of course, a subjective term. But if you are a government minister or a local councillor outraged that your pet project has been described as wasteful, send us a date and time for a public debate and we'll let the taxpayers decide.

So, dear readers, gird your loins because we're going in. *Marvel* at the real examples of waste contained in the following gory pages, *shudder* at the failure to adhere to basic principles of good government, *tremble* at the prospect of these people running your country, and *shriek* with abject terror at where the money is coming from. Because it's your money.

A Brief History of Taxation

550 BC	Croesus invents coinage and makes a mint.
133 BC	Roman Republic inherits the Kingdom of Pergamum, part of Asia Minor. Direct taxation for citizens lifted.
4 BC	Joseph and Mary in Bethlehem to register for tax purposes.
AD 31	Jesus endorses state taxation ("Render unto Caesar the things which are Caesar's").
AD C5	Byzantines develop a complex tax mechanism that pays for a professional army but is a fatal source of dissent. It's all Greek to most people.
1086	Domesday survey. Definitely not a case of self-evaluation.
1283	Edward I starts to build Caernarvon Castle, mimicking Constantinople in style. By 1294 a princely £12,000 has been spent, but there is no north wall facing the town. The Welsh overrun the town and then the castle.
1485	Henry VII comes to the throne. He reforms the tax system. His chancellor, Archbishop Morton, invents 'Morton's fork': if you lived splendidly you had money to waste; if you lived frugally you had money to spare. In both cases you could afford the taxes.
1509	Henry VIII becomes king. Morton's associates, Empson and Dudley, are arrested and then beheaded. Henry VIII is very popular.

1517	Martin Luther and Leo X have a disagreement on Papal finances. The Indulgences of some lead to a Reformation for many.
1568	Tenth Penny tax proposed in the Low Countries, crippling the local economy. It sparks off revolt and the Eighty Years War.
1620s-30s	Charles I tries to impose the Ship Tax to build a fleet. This goes down badly with inland taxpayers. Seeds for Civil War sown.
1698	Peter the Great introduces tax on men with beards. Santa goes into hiding; elves cover for the next 24 years.
1773	Boston Tea Party: US TaxPayers' Alliance launches with the slogan 'No taxation without representation'.
1776	Adam Smith, a son of Edinburgh, publishes *The Wealth of Nations*, a particularly sound work that still inspires supporters to leave pennies on his grave to this day.
1789	French Estates-General meets to sort out the country's tax mess. Englishman Tom Paine joins General Lafayette in participating in what then turns out to be their second Revolution.
1798	Pitt the Younger introduces Income Tax to pay for wars with the French. We still have it today, which says a lot about the state of the *entente cordiale*.
1861	American Civil War begins. One cause is federal tariffs on imported goods and exported cotton, which are unfavourable for the South.

1917   Russian Revolution. Wealth is "redistributed". Dr Zhivago's house is taken over by rude peasants. The country goes down the pan.

1930   Gandhi starts his campaign against the Salt Tax. The era of the Great Hedge of India draws to a close. Gardeners are furious.

1931   Al Capone goes down for tax evasion. Kevin Costner is a happy man in *The Untouchables*, but Sean Connery is turned into Swiss cheese.

1954   VAT invented by Frenchman Maurice Lauré. Bastard.

1973   Britain joins the EEC. Whacky continental tax rules start to kick in.

1994   Mounties and Mohawks in shoot-out over dodging Canadian taxes on smokes.

1997   Stealth taxes enter the national consciousness.

Alfonso Portillo
Former President of Guatemala
c/o Embassy of Guatemala
13 Fawcett Street
London SW10 9HN

December 2005

Dear Mr. Portillo

It has come to our attention that you diverted
millions of dollars of taxpayers' money into
private bank accounts in Panama whilst President
of Guatemala between January 1999 and January
2004. We understand that the sums diverted from
Guatemala's Interior Ministry were as much as
$1.5 million a month.

We are currently compiling a Bumper Book of
Government Waste and we were wondering whether
you could spare the time to comment on whether
you considered these transfers a good use of
taxpayers' money. If you could include a
photograph with your reply for inclusion in the
book we would be grateful.

Thank you in anticipation of your help.

Yours sincerely

Matthew Elliott
TPA Chief Executive

A Brief History of Waste

2560 BC	Pharaoh Khufu builds the Great Pyramid as an imposing sepulchre. It is 480 feet high, is the tallest structure on earth up to the nineteenth century, and takes the local labour force an estimated twenty years to build. His body is still nicked.
404 BC	Artaxerxes II flaunts his bling. His jewellery alone is worth 12,000 talents (about £3 million). Persians give decadence a bad name.
C1 BC	Ostentation in ancient Italy. Cicero complains of plays which use props of six hundred mules or three thousand bowls just to look flash. The sheer costs and rewards of high office encourage corruption, indolence and worse. The era of Bread and Games begins.
AD 64	Great Fire of Rome. Nero builds a Golden Palace on the ruins, covering two of Rome's seven hills, with an artificial lake in the middle. He demolishes an unfinished temple to his uncle to make way for it. A colossal statue to Nero on the site would later give its name to the nearby Colosseum.
193	Pertinax bribes the Praetorians to make him Emperor. He then finds out he can't pay. His head is on a pole within three months, and the habit is made of throwing money at the army to stay alive.

410	Alaric the Goth sacks the Eternal City, then dies. He is buried with his mass of loot and a river is diverted to hide his tomb. Surviving Roman taxpayers are relieved but substantially poorer.
625	King Raedwald buried at Sutton Hoo. A ship is buried with him. Local transport links suffer.
991	Aethelred pays the first Danegeld. The Danes return repeatedly in subsequent years for further pay-offs. More English pennies of this period have been dug up in Denmark than in England.
1194	Blondel de Nesle wanders around Europe singing songs to towers. He eventually finds Richard the Lionheart held captive by the dastardly Austrians. A king's ransom is paid (by the taxpayer, of course).
1511-1525	Henry VIII spends £1,400,000, or twelve years' national income, solely on wars with France. There are no permanent gains and the period ends with tax riots.
1661	First moves by Louis XIV to create the great Palace of Versailles. Estimates of its final running costs vary between 6 per cent and 25 per cent of the income of France. And this ignores his *pied-a-terre* at Marly.
1711	South Sea Trading Company buys £9,000,000 of privatised national debt. Subscribers expect massive inroads into the Spanish Empire in South America, but these do not materialise. Financial collapse follows in the first dot-comtinent scandal.

1864   Ludwig II ascends to the Bavarian throne. One of his aunts is said to have been under the impression she had swallowed a piano made of glass. He lives up to his family's eccentricity, building fabulous Disneyland castles in honour of Wagnerian epics. When royal funds run out and state monies are required to bail him out, he is deposed, and soon found sleeping with the fishes.

1899   Colonial Office and Boers dispute state franchise rights. The resulting conflict lasts almost three years and costs £200 million, requiring mass mobilization of the Empire.

1942   Fall of Singapore to the Imperial Japanese Army. The 'Gibraltar of the Far East' had impressive and expensive sea defences, but was attacked from the land.

1948   British railways nationalised. One cabinet minister later joked that he considered it a personal triumph to have cut the annual loss down to a mere £1 billion in the 1970's.

1959   Britain enters the missile age with Blue Streak. As a nuclear deterrent that takes longer to fire up than a steam engine, its strategic use is limited. It evolves into Black Prince, a multinational satellite launcher. Tony Benn cancels it when French and German bits keep breaking.

1976   Montreal Olympics. Estimated cost: $310 million, final cost: $1.5 billion. Unlike *Expo 67*, the city doesn't even get a new island in the St Lawrence River.

1986	Nimrod early warning aircraft developed to replace WWII radar planes still in use, without buying American. Unfortunately, the radar heats up so much the cockpit melts. The Government buys American.
1989	Basilica of Notre Dame built using public funds in Yamoussoukro, Ivory Coast. It is a (slightly larger) replica of St Peter's of Rome. Great if you like stunning pseudo-Renaissance jungle vistas.
1991	Soviet Union collapses. It has lost the $8 trillion Cold War.
Sept 1992	Black Wednesday. British Government throws £3.3 billion into the system but speculators win the bet that the value of sterling must plummet. At least the lesson keeps us out of the Euro.
New Year's Eve 1999	£1 billion Millenium Dome briefly earns its keep. Queen forced to hold hands with Blairs to sing *Auld Lang Syne*. Surfball makes a temporary bid for the national consciousness.
New Year's Day 2000	The world's computer network decides not to crash due to the Millenium Bug. Start budgeting for the Y2038 problem when the computer clocks wrap around. No excuse for overtime.
2006	No state aid used in the production of this book.

When Mandarin Meets Minister

"So, Minister, you run a government department. Congratulations on your recent appointment. You know what that means, don't you?

Yes! Make a name for yourself and an even better job is yours. Alright, so you can spend a few months in this place sorting out the nation's plumbing issues, fiddling with pensions statistics and the rest. But that won't get you noticed. You need a scheme. What the French would call, *un grand projet.*

President Pompidou built the Pompidou centre - yes the thing with the multicoloured pipes on the outside. Mitterand had the whole Défense area of Paris and the postmodern arch there. Very impressive: you can see it from miles away. De Gaulle had the entire constitution changed. Chirac had, well, some riots. But if you can get a big enough project through the system then you are made.

Cost? Erm . . . don't worry about that. That's what the Chancellor of the Exchequer is there for. Best not to look too closely at this stage. We all know what happens. Department says it wants to spend 40 million. Treasury says you can have 22. Contractor bids for 21. Contract overruns and the Government pays 60. All par for the course. Just don't mention the Scottish Parliament building next time you're in the Treasury. If word gets out, wait for a good day to bury bad news and taxpayers will be none the wiser.

The other thing is, Minister, don't forget that it works both ways. You scratch our back and we scratch yours. Now and again there'll be legislation that comes across your desk. Maybe it's from a colleague, but even better if it comes from Brussels – everybody expects the worst from Brussels. Quite right too. But we have filing cabinets full of legislation that we want to put on the statute book. As soon as anything pops up that looks slightly relevant, we can put in some amendments to the Bill that will increase the workload of our department. Which means, increasing the importance of our department in Whitehall. Which means, Minister, increasing your importance. "Gold plating" is unfair. Makes it sound so, well, grandiose.

It might hurt business a bit, but if that's the price of having an extra hundred people working as departmental inspectors poking their noses in, so be it. Whitehall knows best.

I assume you have read the essays of Cyril Northcote-Parkinson? You know, about the civil service creating more jobs for itself as its responsibilities shrink? How the number of admirals increased with the decline in the numbers of capital ships? The whole business about how we used to run India with fewer people than it takes to run a University these days ? All essential stuff. I'll find a copy for you.

Anyhow, I'll leave you to your red box, Minister. Don't forget your meeting with the Board for the Metrification of Widgets at 3.15."

How the Government Spends Your Money

Total expenditure

Total public spending in 2005-06, according to Treasury figures was around £519 billion – £8,700 for every man, woman and child in the UK. It is set to rise to £549 billion in 2006-07 and to £580 billion in 2007-08.

What it's spent on

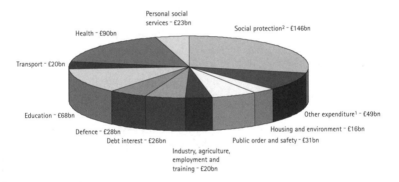

Personal social services – £23bn

Health – £90bn

Social protection[2] – £146bn

Transport – £20bn

Education – £68bn

Defence – £28bn

Debt interest – £26bn

Industry, agriculture, employment and training – £20bn

Public order and safety – £31bn

Housing and environment – £16bn

Other expenditure[1] – £49bn

How much is wasted?

According to our research, £82 billion of the £519 billion is wasted. On the following pages, we show where, how and why.

---

[1] Includes spending on general public services; recreation, culture, media and sport; international co-operation and development; public service pensions; plus spending yet to be allocated and some accounting adjustments.

[2] Social protection includes tax credit payments in excess of an individual's tax liability.

The Taxpayers' Axioms

1. It's not the government's money – it's *your* money.

2. Big government projects always take longer, and cost more, than estimated.

3. Throwing money at a problem is rarely the solution.

4. It is possible to cut taxes and improve services at the same time.

5. If it isn't broke, the civil service will try to mend it.

6. Less regulation means lower costs for business and more jobs.

7. Managers should manage. Government shouldn't waste money on armies of consultants.

8. An ambulance-chasing legal system is a threat to good government.

9. An obsession with lists, targets and quotas distorts priorities and diverts resources away from those who need them.

10. Small gaffes and political correctness add up.

11. The bigger the system gets, the more money it soaks up.

12. Lower taxation creates wealth, which creates more tax revenue, which better supports the needy over the longer term. High taxation does the opposite.

Section Two

Departmental Waste

Plus ça change . . .

In 1974, Prime Minister Harold Wilson sent a memo to his ministers saying,

> "In the coming weeks, I want to show that as a government we are sensitive to little points which may be trivial in the context of government policy but carry a disproportionate weight in people's minds."

Among the "little points" was tax and, in particular, openness with taxpayers on how revenues were being spent. Wilson wrote to his Chancellor, Denis Healey, suggesting that taxpayers should be given a diagram showing how taxes were used.

> "One of the complaints which I often hear from constituents and others is that in contrast to the local rates, no one ever bothers to tell them how their taxes are spent."

He added:

> "I find it hard to believe that the job of putting this extra slip of paper into each envelope would bring the Inland Revenue machine to a halt."

Indeed. Thirty years later, we are still waiting.

Department for Constitutional Affairs

Factoids

Annual expenditure: £3.69 billion (2005-06)

Administration costs: £476 million (2005-06)

Staff: 22,540 [1990: 10,454]

- The DCA currently spends £9 million per year on consultants, compared to £700,000 in 1997. One consultant is paid £2,100 per day.

- In July 2004, the legal aid bill for asylum seekers broke the £200 million per year barrier.

- The DCA's furniture pool is worth an estimated £5 million.

- 6,500 Liverpudlians tried to sue the City Council for tripping over pavements in 2004.

The Department for Constitutional Affairs is a bit of a misnomer. It doesn't spend all its time having a constitutional, and it doesn't organise affairs.

It might, though, be involved in picking up the pieces of some. Take, for example, its £200,000 scheme to help divorcing parents settle custody issues. Unfortunately, only 23 couples came forward to use the service. At that take-up rate, it could have handed out a free car to every loser as a consolation gift.

Basically, the Department for Constitutional Affairs administers the courts and runs legal aid. But if the Government wants to fiddle around with big issue stuff involving your basic Magna Carta-given rights, this is the department that gets to play God.

So what sort of divine activity has it been spending your money on? Let's start with some cracking Old Testament stuff: *retribution.* You may remember the British Government of late has developed a taste for "extraterritoriality". This is about prosecuting criminals from abroad who have done bad things to foreign people in another country. No British citizens are involved either as the accused or as victims, but that doesn't stop the Department for Constitutional Affairs from meddling.

On the one hand, the Crown Prosecution Service has been holding back on prosecuting Iraqis accused of murdering British soldiers through the local courts because they would face the death sentence there. But find any old bad guy in Britain and the Sword of Justice comes crashing down. £3 million was spent prosecuting one Afghan warlord, none of whose victims were British.

Perhaps global justice and the new world order justify expenditure of this magnitude. Less excusable was the money lost on the 2005 Jubilee Line Corruption case, which collapsed leaving a £60 million bill for the taxpayer.

Then there is the money thrown at the Bloody Sunday Inquiry. *The Saville Inquiry* is expected to cost an extraordinary £250 million. To date it has shed no real light on events, but only added further to the discredit of both sides. Even if its existence is justified on the grounds that it heals old wounds, its budget has spiralled wildly, and indecently, out of control.

Runaway expenditure has not entirely escaped the attention of the people who run the DCA. It is now planning to scrap legal aid for divorce battles and medical accidents, saving taxpayers £41 million a year. It should also consider restricting legal aid for asylum seekers, which now costs over £200 million a year. With the total bill for legal aid now exceeding £2 billion, a thorough review is long overdue.

Leading QCs can earn half a million a year from the legal aid fund. Last year, the top ten criminal barristers earned £7.6 million between them. And Cherie Booth, the Prime Minister's wife, pocketed £117,000. Those are pop star wages.

The total Criminal Fund is £1.1 billion a year. Staggeringly, 1 per cent of these cases absorb almost half of all the funds. The result is that the legal aid budget is out of control. The overspend for 2005 is estimated at about £130 million. The shortfall is likely to be taken out on the junior barristers rather than the bigwigs. This in turn may lead to the strange sight of barristers taking the Government's legal supremo to court.

If you think the problem is simply one of a filthy rich, bewigged elite sitting on bags of bullion, think again. The amount of money, including public money, floating around the courts is in part symptomatic of a general shift in Britain towards a blame-and-claim culture.

It doesn't help, of course, that daytime television is awash with adverts telling viewers that if they fall off a ladder into a cauldron of steaming suet, some lawyer on the other end of a phone will take up their case for free.

Prior to the Crown Proceedings Act 1947, you couldn't really sue the state if anything bad happened. Legally, the Crown could do no wrong. As of 1948, the litigation era officially began. It still took until 1987 for section 10 of the Act to be revoked, thus allowing military servicemen to sue for compensation outside of war (like falling down stairs in barracks).

What we now have are two separate types of compensation being awarded. There is, as it were, 'automatic' compensation that the state hands out to people when Fate has metaphorically driven over their picnic in a steamroller. Then there is the type that you get by chasing after the guy who sold the coal to the steamroller in the first place. Naturally, if the state is potentially to blame, so much the better, because it has the biggest reserves of sue-able finances in the country.

We recognise that there are instances where people's lives have been ruined through no fault of their own and for which compensation is appropriate. There are also cases where someone has been a total muppet but has still been compensated by a government department which found it easier to cave in than go to court and fight. Perhaps the most galling aspect of the compensation craze is the total lack of consistency and proportion in the levels of compensation paid out to aggrieved parties.

Compare these awards:

Male nurse does back in while lifting patient	£800,000
Council official "too ill to work due to sexism"	£340,000
Convict falls over in prison shower	£248,000
Fall while umpiring netball match	£77,603
Fall down steps of civil service building	£60,000
Break ankle after slipping on chip	£44,000
Music teacher "overexposed to musical instruments"	£40,000
Gay policemen, compensated for "hurt feelings"	£30,000
Staff member breaks wrist on sports day	£15,000
Boy expelled for bringing a knife to school	£11,000
Whiteboard falls on teacher	£4,550
Fall off "badly positioned chair"	£2,750
Inconvenience to prisoners moved from cells in blaze	£100

to these:

Witness a close family member murdered	£79,000
Lose a limb in a bomb	£55,000
Eye loss	£27,000
Family of child murder victim	£11,000
Husband dies in bombing	£11,000
POW in Burma during WW2 (1951 prices)	£76.50
Gay partner dies in bombing	£0.00
Present at A bomb tests, got cancer but can't prove link	£0.00
Tested on at Porton Down	£0.00
Soldier crippled while on peacekeeping duties	£0.00

Surely shome mishtake?

The insurance industry estimates that the compensation culture costs the country £10 billion a year, of which an estimated £4 billion goes to lawyers. Because so many of the claimants are on legal aid, the public purse – taxpayers' money – funds a sizeable chunk of this.

This will get worse. While it intends to start applying means testing for legal aid, the Government is also planning to lift the half a million pound cap on compensation.

In anticipation, the NHS is reported to have put aside £7.8 billion over the next ten years to cover claims. After all, if the doctor isn't an infallible being with superhuman powers, then he shouldn't be practising medicine, should he? Today, about £500 million is being paid out every year for about 7,000 medical negligence cases. Most observers agree that the valid claims are settled too slowly, so that the legal costs of the smaller claims end up disproportionate to the damages finally awarded.

[The authors would like to take this opportunity to point out to readers that they should not skinny dip in petrol tankers, bungee in a polar bear pit, remove their own kidneys with a spatula, run about screaming Allahu Akbar at JFK Airport, floss with gun cotton, or stick their danglies in an oven on gas mark nine. It hurts, and we accept no responsibility for your utter stupidity.]

The Crown Prosecution Service is another institution that shows an alarming ability to fritter away taxpayers' money. Of course, there are circumstances where a prosecution has to be dropped. Defendants sometimes die before their case gets to court (ideally not by falling down the stairs to the cell, repeatedly). Or the CPS may calculate that the evidence is not strong enough and the chance of conviction too low. Or it might be that Eric the Hatchet turns up late at night and a key witness does a runner.

However, a surprising 17.4 per cent of cases – *one in eight* – that made it to court in the 2004-05 period were subsequently abandoned mid-trial. These included over 2,000 cases where the file was not received from the police, and 1,700 where it was not received from the CPS, and the judge refused to adjourn. Case dismissed because of dog eating homework, perhaps?

Everyone can have a bad day, but nearly *4,000 expensive bad days* seems excessive. Below and over the page are more examples of court cases where the cost to the taxpayer seems to have been totally disproportionate to the outcome.

Case	Cost	Effect
PC uses CS gas on brawling squaddie	£34,000	Case against policeman dropped for lack of evidence
Plane, helicopter and squad car tail woman eating apple whilst driving	£10,000	Apple-eater is fined £60 plus £100 costs

Case	Cost	Effect
Court injunction to provide permanent anonymity for Maxine Carr	£100,000 court case plus estimated £50 million cost of lifetime protection	Cheaper to fly her to Antigua and buy her a mansion
Legal Services support for travellers against Councils and residents	£313,340 on a helpline, £53,000 in legal fees	Embarrassment when minister originally denies funds being used in this way
5 year legal battle over travellers occupying green belt site	£100,000	Landowners finally win after needless wrangling
Challenge over maternity leave underpayment of £204.53	£350,000	Claimant wins, with £65.86 interest
Harold Shipman	£1,180,000 in legal aid	Compares with one of Shipman's now brain-damaged patients who received £225,000

Home Office

Factoids

Annual expenditure: £13.62 billion (2005-06)

Administration costs: £733 million (2005-06)

Staff: 74,010 [1990: 42,721]

- The Home Office spent £74 million in 2004 hiring 142 consultants – a cool half million each.

- £2 million was spent on the massive security operation at the G8 environment meeting in Derbyshire in 2005 where police outnumbered demonstrators by ten to one.

- £250,000 was spent by Sussex Police last year on a 'Facilitating Focus Groups' workshop, a 'Gypsy and Traveller Sites' conference and 198 similar meetings.

- £56,000 of overtime pay was taken home by the top-earning PC in the Met last year.

- Two holistic therapists receive £18,000 a year each for providing inmates in Peterborough Prison with aromatherapy, reiki, reflexology, acupuncture, head massages and shiatsu treatments.

- £11.56 an hour plus expenses is paid to a pagan priest to visit three inmates at Kingston Prison, Portsmouth. To deny them such solace could infringe their human rights, according to the prison governor.

We like coppers. They do a hard job, having to cope with all the paperwork, the rain and the nutcases on the street. On the plus side, they are issued with handcuffs and pepper spray for free, and get to zap felons with taser guns. Fantastic.

Alas, the bureaucrats at the Home Office suffer exactly the same affliction as other mandarins of the public sector when it comes to spending taxpayers' money. Extravagance, waste and incompetence are the norm.

Take, for instance, the money spent hiring consultants to interview 300 drug dealers and smugglers to 'assess the business model of the average drugs dealer'. What's that about?

On a grander scale, consider the flawed and stupendously expensive digital radio system ordered for the country's police forces. The £2.9 billion project for *Airwave* was signed in 2000 and due to be fully operational by the end of 2004.

- The Public Accounts Committee said the system was "more sophisticated and expensive than it really needs to be".

- *Computing* magazine has been told by officers and technical experts that the system only provides limited access to police computer systems and has patchy coverage.

- Police officers have complained of deafness, migraines and nausea after using the equipment.

- There are potential health implications for members of the public living near the 3,350 masts.

- It doesn't work on the Tube.

Sometimes the mis-spending springs from the best of motives. For instance, the Metropolitan Police recently decided to spend £1 million on 'Diversity Advisers'. No one disputes the need to stamp out racism, but there are issues of method and proportionality here. Was £1 million spent on those advisers the best way to do it? The same money would pay for 30 new constables.

London Mayor Ken Livingstone sets the pace when it comes to publicly-funded PC initiatives, but the Met is right behind him. A 2005 conference supported by the Met and by the Association of Chief Police Officers invited a Professor who had supported suicide bombers, including those in Iraq, at an estimated cost of

£9,000. As *The Times* pointed out at the time, they should probably now be arresting themselves for acting in breach of anti-terrorism legislation.

Then there's the ongoing Diana death probe, the bill for which is £2.5 million and growing. *Operation Paget* consists of a team of fifteen led by a former Met chief. £110,000 of this has been spent on expenses, overtime, accommodation, travel and translation, presumably to get across key phrases as "Où est le Ritz, s'il vous plaît?"

The Home Office, though, is not responsible solely for the police. Once you catch a criminal you have to lock him up, which is where the Prison Service comes in. This is a much tougher job, what with constant proximity to hardened criminals but without the thrill of high speed chases through the Isle of Dogs leading to a punch up by some dramatically overturnable dustbins and a "Shut it! We're the Sweeney, son, and we ain't had no breakfast".

Perhaps this explains the 3,000 man-years work that was lost last year, at a cost of £80 million, due to sickness in the prison service. Fair cop, you might say. But the auditors also point to management indifference that has allowed "a culture of pulling sickies" to develop. For instance, one prison officer called in sick for a year . . . from New Zealand. Another staff member pretended to have been run down by a car just before his month long holiday in Sri Lanka was over.

Then there is the mismanagement of asylum seekers. The Government wasted more than £100 million in 2004 keeping 25,000 homes empty for asylum seekers, according to a confidential Downing Street report. A drop in the number of applicants left thousands of homes empty, but the Home Office had to continue to pay rent until June 2005 because they forgot to include an early get-out clause in the contracts. In many cases, it was reported that the rush to get the contracts sorted for these homes meant that the rent was agreed above market rates.

Add to that the National Audit Office's estimate of £300 million as the cost of supporting failed asylum seekers who remain in the country.

And then there was . . .

-   £20 million spent half-building an asylum centre which was then shelved.

-   £874,387 policing the street meetings of Abu Hamza after his mosque had been closed down.

-   £500,000 overtime for six policemen to come in on their days off to man speed cameras.

-   £300,000 for the Met Chief to revamp his office.

-   £205,000 for new central heating to police cells that might drop to 18 degrees Centigrade.

-   £150,000 spent on art for the new Home Office building.

-   The £67,000 salary for Greater Manchester's 'Police Diversity Czar'.

-   £5,000 for two Met officers to visit the San Francisco Gay Pride festival to study community relations.

Taxman

Let me tell you how it will be
There's one for you, nineteen for me
'Cause I'm the taxman, yeah, I'm the taxman

Should five per cent appear too small
Be thankful I don't take it all
'Cause I'm the taxman, yeah I'm the taxman

If you drive a car, I'll tax the street
If you try to sit, I'll tax your seat
If you get too cold, I'll tax the heat
If you take a walk, I'll tax your feet
Taxman

'Cause I'm the taxman, yeah I'm the taxman

Don't ask me what I want it for (Ah ah Mister Wilson)
If you don't want to pay some more (Ah ah Mister Heath)
'Cause I'm the taxman, yeah, I'm the taxman

Now my advice for those who die (Taxman)
Declare the pennies on your eyes (Taxman)
'Cause I'm the taxman, yeah, I'm the taxman
And you're working for no one but me
Taxman

The Beatles (George Harrison)

In July 2004, the Secretary of State for Culture was given a boxed set of Beatles CDs by the Chairman of EMI.

Department for Culture, Media and Sport

Factoids

Expenditure limit: £1.54 billion (2005-06)

Administration budget: £49 million (2005-06)

Staff: 760 [1998: 601]

- £6.8 million was spent by the DCMS building an 84-mile walkers trail along Hadrian's Wall. It is now attracting so many ramblers that the UNESCO site is being eroded and destroyed.

- £2.9 million is the estimated value of the DCMS's *Inn the Park* restaurant in St James's Park where a meal for two with wine and service will set you back £60.

- £240,000 has been written off by the DCMS for art that was lost in a theft in Buenos Aires. The ambassador's temporary residence got burgled by a David Niven wannabe.

- £20,000 of damage was caused over a one year period to the Public Arts Collection.

Modern; ancient; performance; canvas: like it or loathe it, from priceless Old Masters to modern 'installations', from fat German valkyries to graceful anorexics dying like swans, from intricate sculptures to piles of elephant dung, we, the taxpayers, sponsor the art we see around us.

The Department for Culture, Media and Sport looks after eight royal parks and directly supports 24 museums. The DCMS itself is quite small, but it supervises organisations which hand over huge amounts of our money in arts, sports and film grants. Like most departments, the head civil servant earns twice as much as the Secretary of State who is her boss.

Many of the grants are directed through a quango called the Arts Council. This august institution has a budget of around a billion pounds a year, and a correspondingly casual attitude to spending it. Consider some of the recent beneficiaries of its largesse.

- £7,000 was spent sending four teachers on a cultural exchange to Hawaii.

- In 2003, a lecturer was paid £12,000 to kick an empty curry carton down the street.

- A local artists group in Birmingham received £15,000 from the Arts Council for a study of the City's changing drinking habits. The project involved spending six hours in five pubs in a single afternoon. The cash paid for food, entertainment and information packs for the artists and the thirty members of the public who joined them. Students normally have to dodge lessons to be that dedicated.

When in 2005 the Public Accounts Committee examined fifteen projects such as these, thirteen were found to be over budget, and eight behind schedule. It is not clear if alcohol poisoning was responsible.

On the subject of alcohol, one has to hand it to the Japanese artist who last year persuaded the Arts Council to part with £5,000 to support her performance art. This involved drinking 48 pints of lager then trying to cross a beam in high heels and a business suit. Disappointingly, the 48 pints were symbolic and not all of them were consumed. What a missed opportunity, though: wheeled off with a broken leg, she'd have been able to get even more money out of the Arts Council by suing it for negligence.

There's also the £800,000 ladled out from the National Art Collection's Fund to turn an 18th century shed into a place where people can peer through a hole in the roof and contemplate the sky. In many parts of the country, the same money would buy an entire street of terraced houses with outdoor privies.

[The authors would like to disassociate themselves from any real criticism of the wonderful work the Arts Council and other similar bodies are undertaking, and hope it does not prejudice their bid for funds to support their pending oeuvre, 'Midnight jet skiing on the Serpentine with ten bottles of Krug'.]

The British Council has also shown itself prone to astonishing lapses of judgment when it comes to disbursing public funds, notably in using part of its £180 million budget not to promote Britain's place in the world, but to actually do the country down.

Which patriot, one wonders, decided it would be a good use of taxpayers' money to sponsor a photographic exhibition in the

Middle East that portrayed Muslims living in the UK as victims of an unfriendly culture. One shot portrayed an ethnic group underneath some racist graffiti.

Similarly, the Council was forced to apologise and remove from its website an article which claimed that UK policy in Iraq was to use it as a testing ground for cluster bombs. And another one which attacked Israel. Fine as an op-ed in a left-leaning newspaper, but hardly appropriate for taxpayer-funded material, particularly as it seems to breach anti-discrimination laws.

Other examples of DCMS extravagance include the £77,000 spent sending a team of artists to the North Pole to make a snowman, and the Princess Diana memorial fountain. Originally costed at an already exorbitant £3.6 million, the final bill for the memorial is now expected to exceed £5 million, with a staggering annual maintenance bill of £200,000. For that price you could afford to buy three brand new Renault Premium 420.25 articulated lorries, load the trailers to the brim with rubber ducks and float them in the water as performance art.

So much for art. The DCMS also covers **media and sport,** which means that the BBC falls under its wing. And, as you might expect from an organisation that advertises for staff in the *Guardian*, there is an element of almost ministerial disregard for taxpayers' money in this public institution as well.

Some of the waste is due to the BBC's Government-inspired policy of using outside contractors. Take the property management company that was reported in 2005 to have charged the Corporation £57 to change a light bulb, and £2,500 to put up nine shelves.

On other occasions, the profligacy is just an attempt to be trendy, as when the BBC paid £60,000 for a Tracey Emin bronze bird on a pole outside one of its offices. Leaks later revealed the BBC had difficulty inventing an excuse for buying it.

The Government itself has spent four times that – £240,000 – on an expensive language course. That's the cost (so far) of supporting the Cornish language in schools, on dual language signs, on town signs and in publications. As it happens, there are an estimated 500 competent Cornish speakers nationwide, which means the grant would have been enough to buy each of them an entire shelf of books and videos, for a language that speakers have to specially congregate in pubs to use. One in eight are said to live in London (a city incidentally which last heard spoken Cornish around AD 500).

If one was feeling exceptionally generous, a quarter of a million pounds to support Cornish could just about be justified on the grounds that it invigorates the language gene pool. The sums due to be spent on the 2012 London Olympics are on another scale altogether and, for taxpayers, quite chilling.

Consider Greece's experience as host of the 2004 Games. The credit rating of the entire country dropped as a result of the public money sunk into the event and its inevitable overspend. In the process, Greece breached the rules for membership of the Euro zone.

How much the 2012 Olympics will cost taxpayers is a question which supporters of the Games seem strangely reluctant to discuss. The threat on just the current calculation alone is that the average council tax bill in London will go up by £20 a year for a decade. China, which is hosting the next Games, is reportedly budgeting £23 billion, which is way above anything the London organisers have been prepared to admit.

To put that figure in context, it costs about £1,000 to equip, train and employ an Iraqi for a year to look after one of the ancient historical sites of Mesopotamia that are currently being trashed on a regular basis by looters. £23 billion would employ 10,000 guards on double pay for a thousand years.

And then there was . . .

- £30 million underwriting the Contemporary Art Gallery in Margate, which is currently running at over four times its estimate cost.

- £400,000 spent on 50 works of art for British embassies, including pictures of plastic bags and drawings made from mud.

- £48,000 of Lottery money spent on a 'traveller culture' DVD for schools.

- £31,000 spent on a satellite sports channels for civil servants.

Department of Health

Factoids

Annual expenditure: £78.24 billion (2005-06)

Administration costs: £303 million (2005-06)

Departmental Staff: 6,750 [1990: 5,422]

- £400 million is spent by the NHS on anti-depressants in England every year – almost fifteen times more than was spent twenty years ago.

- In 2004, the NHS spent £85 million on consultants.

- The average GP earns £100,000+ per year, double the figure of six years ago.

- The average full-time NHS dentist earns £80,000 per year.

- For every £100 invested in the NHS, £56 is swallowed up by higher wages and administration. Another £9 is lost through poor productivity.

- There were 121,000 administrators in the NHS in 2004 – up by a fifth in two years. These additional suits cost half a billion pounds and could have paid for 27,000 nurses.

Nurses are hard-working, do icky jobs and are not terribly well paid. Beyond criticism, in fact. But taxpayers who care one iota about the medical bang they get for their buck have to take a stand against the waste within the National Health Service.

The NHS is the biggest employer in Europe and third only in the world to Indian Railways and the Chinese Red Army. Despite the sums of money being pumped into healthcare in the United Kingdom, the problems with the NHS are seemingly intractable. Spending since 1997 has doubled but the level of improvements in the system has not.

Why is this?

A 2004 report, commissioned by the Office for National Statistics and led by Professor Sir Tony Atkinson, suggests that the NHS may be wasting up to £6 billion a year as rising inefficiency reduces NHS productivity. That's the staggering equivalent of about 250,000 new nurses.

While real resources to the NHS rose by somewhere between 32 to 39 per cent between 1995 and 2003, after allowing for inflation in its pay and costs, the output of services to patients has increased by just 28 per cent. This gap is the £6 billion lost through falling productivity.

Nor do the NHS Trusts that handle all the newly invested money seem capable of doing so efficiently. One in three is in deficit and being forced to make an estimated £1 billion in cutbacks, including ward closures.

Then there is the vexed question of targets. Managerial goal-setting has a disturbing tendency to distort clinical priorities, with fiddles, like creating lists to get on lists, being used to mask problems.

The waiting list system has resulted in less serious cases being prioritised in order to meet targets. One case proves the book-balancing point: the leading orthopaedic surgeon at Chase Farm Hospital in Enfield handed in his notice after 30 years in the NHS, because "all managers care about is not breaching targets". The surgeon said he was told to treat routine bunion operations ahead of elderly emergency patients with fractured hips.

Despite his protests that elderly patients awaiting hip operations were suffering and gradually dying – the waiting time for an emergency fracture has gone up from two to eight days – he claims the Trust's Chief Executive told him to treat waiting list patients first to ensure that the hospital met its targets. This was despite the fact that he had patients with fractured hips, pre-deep vein thrombosis and pressure sores who were losing the will to live because they were in so much pain.

A perfect example of The Law of Unintended Consequences occurred when the Government stipulated a few years ago that GPs should see all patients within 48 hours of the request for an appointment. Incentivised financially to meet this target, practices all over the country did the obvious thing: they forbade patients from making appointments more than 48 hours before a vacant slot.

The unintended but entirely predictable consequence was that a patient could not make an appointment on Monday to see her doctor on Friday. Instead she, and any other patients who wanted a Friday appointment, had to wait until Wednesday and hope that they were the first ones through when the phone lines opened. It was a nonsensical and inefficient booking system brought about by well-meaning but misguided government interference.

Perhaps most worrying of all was that Tony Blair knew nothing about this problem until he was harangued by a member of the audience on the BBC's *Question Time* in April 2005. GPs had long been complaining that the target system was bad for patients, but the Government took no notice. If the driving force of NHS reform is so out of touch with the situation on the ground, is it surprising that the reforms have been so unsuccessful?

Inefficiency in the NHS is much more serious than financial loss, of course. It can be terminal. According to the National Audit Office, the cost of hospital-acquired infections to the NHS is as much as £1 billion per year. Apart from the direct financial cost, the health risks in hospitals are appalling. Whatever the origin of the MRSA problem – poor management, private cleaning contractors, the removal of autonomy for matrons – it is clearly unacceptable for the country to have an MRSA problem that is worse than any of its European counterparts.

Let's look at other specific instances of waste within the NHS.

Recruitment

Some waste is due to the way the NHS managers employ staff. The Department for Health has spent £53 million setting up a state sector organisation to supply agency staff to the NHS, but there is no evidence that it has succeeded. NHS Professionals cost taxpayers £22 million in 2003-04, but spending on temporary doctors and nurses has risen every year since Labour came to power, reaching £1.6 billion last year. Obviously, temps cost more over the long term than recruiting and keeping your own staff, so this is more money down the drain.

Litigation

The Department of Health is particularly vulnerable to negligence lawsuits, because medical procedures always carry some risk and the consequences of failure can be catastrophic. Clinical negligence claims against the NHS currently run at £5.89 billion a year, according to the National Audit Office, and could be as high as £9 billion.

It might help if the walls of hospital waiting rooms were not plastered with advertisements from law firms encouraging patients to sue. By improving NHS delivery along recommended lines and restricting frivolous compensation claims, the Department could easily halve the amount of compensation it pays out and save taxpayers £3 billion.

Hospital Planning

A brief example of a hospital planning disaster: the NHS Paddington Basin super-hospital merger.

The hospital should have been running by early 2006 but by late 2005 the merger planners hadn't even bought the land, let alone been granted planning permission. When the land price leapt by

£30 million, the viability of the project started to unravel. To make up for spiralling costs, projected bed numbers were cut from 1,088 to 799. £7 million was spent on external consultants. Bad went to worse, and in the end, the planners were forced to cancel the entire project. The lost money, estimated at £14 million, would have paid for 800 heart bypass operations.

Health Tourism

'Health Tourism' costs the UK taxpayer an estimated £200 million per year. The term doesn't mean weekends in a swanky Helsinki sauna. It is the costly practice whereby 100,000 people from overseas visit the UK every year to take advantage of free hospital treatment. Some estimates put the cost as high as £2 *billion* a year. Either way, British taxpayers are losing twice: once to pay for the Health Tourist and then – irony of ironies – a second time to pay for patients who are sent by the NHS for treatment abroad to reduce waiting lists.

Missed Appointments

The simplest of failings – not turning up at the surgery – and this time patients must take the rap. The fact is, millions of NHS appointments are missed every year. On average, patients fail to turn up to nine million GP appointments and four million nurse appointments, according to the health charity *Developing Patient Partnerships*. This costs the NHS at least £575 million a year. Polls of GPs show that 68 per cent support the idea of fining patients for missing appointments. Others have suggested charging patients £5 to see their GP.

Consider what would happen if appointments carried a £5 motivating charge, refundable if the patient turns up. It would cut the waste massively. Of course, the cancellation phone lines would need to be manned, which isn't always the case at the moment.

The Public Accounts Committee has come up with some very specific observations on the Ulster NHS. It noted that over a third of available weekday theatre capacity was not being used, with little use of theatres in the evenings and weekends. This has to be viewed in the context of Northern Ireland's waiting lists and waiting times for treatment, which are currently the worst in the United Kingdom, and the spending in Northern Ireland on acute health services, which has been higher than in England. Better use of operating theatres there would contribute to reducing the length of time that patients have to wait for treatment.

Ghost Patients

GP practices are paid by the NHS through a formula partly based on the number of patients on their lists and their age range. The more elderly patients a practice has, the more money it receives. According to a 2004 Audit Commission report, £100 million a year is being spent on 'ghost patients' who, despite having died or moved out of the area, remain on the surgery's list. The Commission estimates that there are at least 3.5 million excess names on GP lists in England alone. Jolly nice for GPs. Not so good for taxpayers.

There have also been cases reported of lists being manipulated to remove certain categories of patients when funding suits the practitioner. There is clearly money to be saved by stamping out that kind of thing.

Unused Repeat Prescriptions

North Warwickshire Primary Care Trust recently reported that £1 million of its £28 million annual drugs bill is wasted because repeat prescriptions are not being properly managed.

This is a widespread problem. The NHS spends well over £6 billion a year on prescriptions. If the Warwickshire figures are representative of all Trusts, £214 million is being chucked away on unused repeat prescriptions.

'Useless' NRT

The NHS spends over £50 million a year on nicotine patches and gums despite new evidence that they do not help smokers to quit the habit. A Treasury report questioned the success rates that supposedly justify the use of nicotine replacement therapy in clinics. Besides, the patches don't light so easily.

Staff Suspensions

Money could also be saved in the way NHS staff suspensions are handled. The Public Accounts Committee has called on the Government to reduce the number of NHS staff suspended from work, after it found that suspensions were costing £40 million a year. Reducing this figure by speeding up the tribunal process could save taxpayers a substantial proportion of this.

Overview of NHS Productivity

The think tank *Reform* has pioneered the analysis of NHS productivity by comparing the growth in the numbers of waiting list patients treated with the growth in the overall NHS budget. For example, between 1999-2000 and 2003-04, the number of waiting list patients treated per year rose by 11.0 per cent compared to an increase in the overall budget of 31.1 per cent in real terms.

Ministers and senior NHS officials responded that these types of estimates are inaccurate since they did not include NHS activity outside hospitals. In October 2004, the Office of National Statistics produced new figures stemming from additional work by the Atkinson Review team and covering over three quarters of all NHS activity. This showed that NHS productivity has fallen by up to 1 per cent per year since 1997.

The NHS, quite simply, needs a massive overhaul rather than being managed into the ground. It could start with hospitals reviewing their priorities. University College Hospital has spent £70,000 on a big polished rock. Other hospitals have spent £35,000 on a mural, £18,000 on textile roof hangings, and £3,000 on a sculpture of 300 birds. The total reported spend on hospital art over two years was £9 million. University College Hospital has hired an art curator on a salary of £40,000 a year. Royal London Hospital hired one as well, on £36,000 a year. Another NHS Trust hired someone part-time on a nurse's wages as a Trolley Art Project Manager.

And then there was . . .

- The NHS spent £40,000 on a 46-word 'Patient Experience Definition' defining what makes a good experience for a patient. This presumably excluded anything to do with abuse of opiates. Following two £8,000 workshops with patients, a £4,000 public meeting, two £1,600 meetings with children and three £600 in-depth interviews with mental patients, they received a definition which stated the bleedin' obvious:

  "Getting good treatment in a comfortable, caring and safe environment, delivered in a calm and reassuring way; having information to make choices, to feel confident and to feel in control; being talked to and listened to as an equal; being treated with honesty, respect and dignity."

  The Department of Health said that, "We now plan to use the Definition to improve the patient experience".

- The Department of Health is spending £225,000 on workshops that include teaching old people how not to fall over. Some of these are "sloppy slipper events" – teaching grannies about ill-fitting slippers. Ministers have described the scheme as "pioneering" and health experts claim a saving of £1.8 million as a result of those who learnt not to fall over. The initiative has been greeted with scorn by pensioners' groups. The Chairman of Islington Pensioners' Forum said: "It's patronising. You can't teach your grandmother to suck eggs and neither can you teach her how to wear her slippers."

- An extra £1.5 billion a year has been spent on backroom management every year since the mid 1990s.

- The NHS is spending £2 million a year on computer training for porters and cleaners, after deciding to offer the EU's Computer Driving Licence to all staff irrespective of their position. In 2004, over three million hours of tuition was provided, suggesting that the real cost of the scheme could be far higher than the £2 million claimed. In man hours alone, £30 million could have been wasted, based on the average NHS salary of almost £10 an hour. When his cleaner took the course, one doctor quipped: "At long last she will be able to calculate the optimal path for her vacuum cleaner."

- £1 million was spent in 2005 to protect Ken Livingstone and his employees from the bird flu pandemic. BBC staff are also on the Government's priority list. So too are senior ministers. But not, obviously, the Opposition.

- £900,000 was been spent in 2005 on market research to find out what the public want from GPs.

- In the same year, £500,000 was splashed out on an EU health ministers' meeting, while a local hospital closed two wards.

- £100,000 was spent on leaflets warning people to stay out of the sun.

Foreign and Commonwealth Office

Factoids

Annual expenditure: £1.8 billion (2005-06)

Administration costs: £798 million (2005-06)

Staff: 6,050

- Britain has 10 per cent more diplomats than five years ago.

- £295,500 was spent last year by the Government Art Collection on art, mostly for hanging in overseas embassies.

- £38,000 was paid out by the FCO in 2004-05 for two cases of repetitive strain injury.

- £22,000 was paid out to someone who got a burn injury at an embassy function.

- £12,150 was spent by the FCO in 2005 on logos.

The Foreign and Commonwealth Office: the face of Britain overseas. The Rolls-Royce of the civil service? Well, certainly when it comes to some of the costs involved.

The taxpayer is forking out a staggering £100 million for MoD and FCO staff to send their children to top public schools charging fees of up to £22,000 per child per year. This is happening under the same government that scrapped the assisted places scheme to help children from poorer backgrounds attend these same schools through scholarships. A strange case of double standards.

There is, admittedly, some logic to many of these civil servants getting support to offload their kids, because a number of them have to scoot off to Kabul and the local comprehensives there aren't too good. But there are decent boarding schools costing a third of the amount charged by the top-notch public schools. And since the scheme also includes UK-based staff, it looks more like a perk at taxpayers' expense than a genuine requirement of office.

The FCO also has at its disposal 40,000 bottles of rather nice wine, worth around £3 million. Some £100,000 of new stock is regularly 'laid down' for future generations of thirsty FCO staff. You and I would nip out to Oddbins, but no, that would not do for the discriminating oenophiles in Whitehall. Their experts meet four times a year for tastings.

The Department, as the face of Britain, obviously has to impress its guests. That's why the embassies forsake the attractions of Ikea, and choose instead to put some of the nation's most precious assets on display. Our embassy in Washington has a set of silver worth £485,000. In Istanbul there are two chandeliers valued at £350,000. In Havana, there is a rug valued at £130,000.

We didn't just fall off the turnip truck. We know that sumptuous extravagance on this scale is part and parcel of competing on the diplomatic circuit with the vainglorious French. And if the antique furnishings and art that grace our embassy reception rooms have been owned by the nation for centuries, then at least there is no capital cost to taxpayers. What is harder to stomach is the spending of public money to the tune of £175,000 on a Damien Hirst which the public will never get to see. The piece was sent to Brussels, and then probably on to an embassy as a conversation piece for cocktail parties. The copyright terms mean that even photos of it can't be seen.

For sheer comedy value, let's round things off with the case of the Thuraya satellite phone that the Foreign Office somehow lost in the Middle East. The FCO subsequently received a phone bill of half a million pounds, after someone in Iraq used the stolen phone to ring up Yemen and Saudi Arabia. Bin Laden, incidentally, remains unaccounted for.

Kim Jong-il
President
Democratic People's
  Republic of Korea
c/o DPR Korea Embassy
73 Gunnersbury Avenue
London W5 4LP
December 2005

Dear President Jong-il,

We are currently compiling a Bumper Book of
Government Waste and were wondering if you would
be so kind as to give us your comments on the
following points.

First of all, we have read that you employ a
nubile "Pleasure Squad" of young Asians and
Europeans to help you relax. Do you pay for this
from your own salary as President of North Korea
or is it a "perk of the job" to help you
concentrate on your work? If it is the latter, is
it taxable and, if so, what is its taxable value?

Secondly, we understand that you have a fortune
of $4 billion and that the GDP of the Democratic
People's Republic of Korea is $40 billion. As
Korea's biggest taxpayer, have you considered
setting up a North Korean TaxPayers' Alliance?

Thank you in anticipation of your help.

Yours sincerely

TPA Chief Executive

P.S. Might it be possible for us to interview the
"Pleasure Squad"?

Department for Transport

Factoids

Annual expenditure: £11.74 million (2005-06)

Administration costs: £242 million (2005-06)

Staff: 17,150

- The DfT's biggest asset is the 'Trunk Road Network', estimated value – £72 billion.

- Its second biggest asset, the Channel Tunnel Rail Link, is valued at £1.5 billion.

- £36 million worth of land at Dartford is owned by the DfT.

- £888,000 would buy you what is probably the most expensive vehicle on British roads – the Department's road inspection vehicle – making it even more expensive than the original Batmobile, or ten Aston Martins.

- 62 bypasses have been built since 1997, 13 of them in marginal constituencies. This is entirely and absolutely coincidental, including the one built in the Prime Minister's own constituency.

"Bing Bong. The 9:27 to Huddersfield has been cancelled. We would like to apologise for any inconvenience this might cause you. *Bing Bong."*

Ah, happy days. The time of yore when British rail was British Rail, the pork pies came with a Government health warning, and excuses like "leaves on the line" were for wimps.

A lot of money is being invested in public transport and the Government is very proud of it. **The Railway network alone sucks up £87 million of taxpayers' money a week**, with the biggest ever improvement in, and refurbishment of, rolling stock in recent history. We have the fastest growing railway in Europe, with more than one billion passenger journeys last year.

Well, that's the Government version. But look at the following graph produced by the Department for Transport:

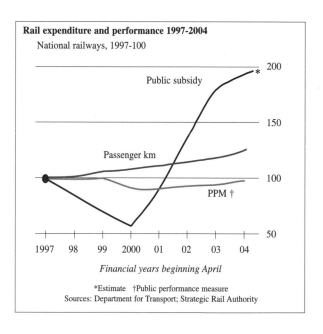

Rail expenditure and performance 1997-2004

National railways, 1997-100

Financial years beginning April

*Estimate   †Public performance measure
Sources: Department for Transport; Strategic Rail Authority

The graph shows three things:

1. How much people are using the railways.
2. How well the railways are performing.
3. How much money is going in to subsidise it.

The story it tells has two distinct phases:

- From 1997-2000, the Government cut back heavily on investment. The quality of service dropped but not by much.

- From 2000 onwards the Government threw wads of money at the problem, but standards barely improved, and the number of rail passengers was largely unaffected.

On the right-hand side of the graph, you can see that record money is currently being spent on the railways, but passenger usage and service standards are lagging badly. The issue is not whether or not the railway network needed investment. Clearly it did. The issue is whether *so much* needed to be spent and whether what has been spent was spent *wisely*.

On that, we must turn to the Government's Rail Regulator who, in his December 2003 report, said that more than £1 billion of Network Rail's annual spending was work "that the company does not need to do" and a further £1.5 billion could be saved "by eliminating waste and inefficiency". £2.5 billion of wasteful spending is a conservative estimate because, according to the NAO, the Strategic Rail Authority has set aside £3 billion to cover overspending this year.

Now that's a budget that's gone entirely off the rails.

And then there was . . .

- Network Rail's debt of £17 billion. This is not included in the national debt because Network Rail claims to be an independent company. Debt markets therefore charge it a higher interest rate, adding £30 million a year to its annual interest bill.

- £10.5 million spent developing tram systems for British cities, before the Department got cold feet and backed out. The projects faltered.

- £140,000 spent on the upkeep of London transport supreme Bob Kiley's house. When it was bought by Transport for London five years ago, it was said to have been "restored and modernised to an exceptionally high standard".

- Bob Kiley also invoiced London taxpayers £2,594.99 to cover one dinner party for 22 people. At almost £120 per head, it would have been cheaper to take them to The Ritz.

Department for Education and Skills

Factoids

Annual expenditure: £30.72 billion (2005-06)

Administration costs: £275 million (2005-06)

Staff: 5,450 [1990: 2,560]

- 2,500 people work in the Office for Standards in Education.

- £70 million was spent by the Learning and Skills Council in 2004 alone hiring 135 consultants – an average of half a million each.

- A 58 per cent increase in spending on education over the past eight years has barely improved standards.

- A 15-20 per cent decrease in efficiency has occurred in the same period according to official statistics.

Like healthcare professionals, teachers have been whacked by bureaucracy. The red tape that came with extra government money has seen too much of the funds sidelined or swamped.

The Office of National Statistics has published its estimate of "school-level education productivity". Old figures had shown that productivity had fallen on average by 2 per cent per year since 1998. Even after rejigging the figures to take account of a change in the overall number of pupils, the ONS confirmed that the productivity of state education has still fallen overall. Indeed, it has mirrored the decline in productivity, pound for pound, of the NHS.

Some waste has been through pointless schemes. The **truancy campaign** has been written off as a waste of £1 billion and hundreds of hours of police time, say two independent reports. Even after ten years of failed schemes, 70,000 pupils still skip school on any given weekday. The Government on election pledged to cut rates by a third; truancy figures have in fact gone up by two fifths.

There are also the **teachers who never teach**. According to House of Commons Public Accounts Committee member Richard Bacon MP, taxpayers spend £100 million each year training teachers who never set foot in the classroom. After qualifying, they decide they don't want to teach after all. Such poor levels of retention by the DfES amount to £100 million down the drain.

For a one-off example of breathtakingly arrogant government spending, it is difficult to beat UKeU, the online university which gobbled its way through £62 million. UKeU was set up in 2000 with the aim of attracting overseas students to study online with UK universities. Its £2 million-plus wage bill for 2002-03 included a £180,000 salary for the Chief Executive, who also received a performance-related bonus that year of £44,914. This despite the fact that UKeU attracted just 900 students over four years at a cost to the taxpayer of £44,000 each. After a highly critical review by PA Consulting in 2003,

UKeU responded to the report by – *wait for it* – asking for a further £15 million!

Dr Ian Gibson MP, Labour Chairman of the House of Commons Science and Technology Committee which investigated the UkeU scandal, described it as "a shameful waste of tens of millions of pounds, an absolute disaster". The project was eventually put to the sword in late 2004.

Some of the **academic studies** which are funded by public money beggar belief. Academics from London Metropolitan University carried out a £7,000 study into four strip clubs in Glasgow. The team studied the entertainment provided at the city's Truffle Club, Legs and Co, Diamond Dolls and Seventh Heaven.

Other university researchers spent three years and a hefty £140,000 of taxpayers' money visiting a range of cafés. One specialised in gathering data on such delights as cake and hazelnut frappucinos. The report concluded with a series of observations that were blindingly perceptive, such as "people will stop going if the coffee is not so good", and "asking if you can borrow a paper from someone may lead to a cold shoulder or a warm response". Someone in the Department should have woken up and smelled the coffee on that one.

But then, who guards the guards? As part of the refurbishment of the Ofsted offices, the DfES bought wallpaper costing £1,100 a roll! £35,000 was spent on ten giant plasma televisions. Potted plants came in at £500 a throw. The Bristol office is to get three shower rooms with Italian mosaic tiles, not forgetting the nineteen solid oak doors imported from America.

Compensation claims are also a growing problem in the education sector. Former Cabinet Minister Stephen Byers has criticised the compensation culture hitting the public sector in which "the real beneficiaries are the lawyers and accident management companies". Compensation claims against schools total £200 million – funds that could pay for 8,000 new teachers, 22,700 nurses or go towards lower taxes.

And then there was . . .

- £400 million spent on a project to encourage kids from poor backgrounds to apply for university. The DfES's own report admitted that it had had little effect.

- £10 million spent on a scheme to teach pupils how to be "nice".

- £1 million blown on a sports hall that was later demolished to make way for an identical million-pound sports hall, to save the school paying a massive VAT bill on extensions.

- £27,500 allocated to a research project comparing the human soul to car mechanics.

- A £100,000 research grant made to a scientist to investigate if people are telepathic. *Are you thinking what we're thinking?*

Department of Trade and Industry

Factoids

Annual expenditure: £6.1 billion (2005-06)

Administration costs: £454 million (2005-06)

Staff: 12,580 [1990: 11,793]

- £30,000 was spent last year by the DTI on renaming itself the Department for Productivity, Energy and Industry. Six days later, the resulting jokes about the rude acronym led to a swift reversal.

- £90 is the average bill per person at the smart London restaurant *Pont de la Tour* where a group of eleven DTI officials enjoyed dinner at public expense.

- 23 gin and tonics, 14 vodka and tonics, 3 mojitos and 3 shots of whisky were paid for using a Government credit card at one DTI social.

Once again, the Department of Trade and Industry is a misnomer. Given the amount of paperwork and regulation it churns out, it should be called the Department *against* Trade and Industry. The Government spends over £12 billion a year regulating our lives and business activities, much of it through the DTI.

The DTI is like an 80 foot blancmange in your back garden: it costs a lot, seeps everywhere and serves little purpose. Academics and accountants have openly doubted the usefulness of the DTI. The value of **Research Councils** – a key part of the DTI's activity – has been questioned by leading academic Tim Ambler, Senior Fellow of the London Business School. Posing the question "Do research councils deliver or are we simply looking at jobs for the boys?" he went on to conclude that:

"The British taxpayers could probably save themselves a billion pounds a year at no detriment to productivity or quality of life by dispensing with research councils altogether."

Other research suggests that the DTI has failed to support technology businesses – a key sector of the service economy. Leading accountants Grant Thornton said in 2003:

"95% of DTI funds, supposedly earmarked to support business, may actually fail to reach technology companies, according to research commissioned by business and financial advisers."

To their credit, unlike Labour and the Tories, the Liberal Democrats have recognised that the DTI is a waste of money and are calling for its abolition.

According to Lib Dem Treasury spokesman Vince Cable, "both business and consumers would be better served if the department was abolished". It is estimated by the Liberal Democrats that abolishing the DTI itself would save £5 billion.

When even the Lib Dems – not known for their zeal in cutting government spending – question a department's usefulness, it's a cut-and-dry case.

And then there was . . .

- The £7.5 billion Sick Miners' Fund compensation scheme. Excessive amounts were swallowed in Union lawyers' legal fees, resulting in a police enquiry.

- The £2 billion Regional Development Agencies whose strategies are, to use the technical term favoured by a former government adviser and Managing Director of the Cambridge Innovation Centre, "arse about face".

- £5 million per building for the Small Business Incubation Centres said to be set up "without any real understanding of what they will achieve".

"Government's view of the economy could be summed up in a few short phrases: If it moves, tax it. If it keeps moving, regulate it. If it stops moving, subsidise it."

Ronald Reagan

Department for Environment, Food and Rural Affairs

Factoids

Annual expenditure: £3.23 billion (2005-06)

Administration costs: £317 million (2005-06)

Staff: 14,480

- £3.5 billion is the estimated cumulative cost of BSE.

- The top ten forests owned by the Forestry Commission are valued at £168 million. Half of this is accounted for by the 230 square miles of Kielder Forest.

- £500,000 was given to one airline catering business under the Common Agricultural Policy for "exporting" sugar sachets and little milk containers that were served on planes.

- £2,626 was sent to Eton College from the Rural Payments Agency last year for its playing fields. No one knew why.

- 23,000 farms kept dairy cows in Britain in 2002 (the latest year for which figures are available) compared to 38,000 in 1990. With over 14,000 civil servants working for DEFRA, we now have a ratio of one civil servant to one hundred dairy cows in the UK.

- Six of the top ten departmental compensation handouts were personal injury claims from the foot and mouth epidemic.

Ah, the countryside. The rugged wolds, the sweet green valleys, the prancing lambs, the gentle whoosh of the wind farm . . .

It has been estimated by experts that the real cost of **wind production** require £12 billion of state subsidies by 2015, or three times the cost of supporting nuclear power. The problem is that the network needs adapting to cater for the unpredictability of it being a bit gusty. Plus there's the issue of modifying the land around the wind farm so you can drive a hoofing great truck up to the site to deliver all the parts and put them up. This could add an extra £1 billion a year to electricity prices.

Of course, there are political considerations about choosing whether to go windy. Wind farms are certainly much less dangerous than nuclear plants if terrorists ever hijack them. "One false move and Melton Mowbray's kettles get it!" But the total cost of all the alternative energy sources should be tallied up or the taxpayer will be paying through the nose for years to come.

The Common Agricultural Policy

DEFRA is the department responsible, at face value, for handling the Common Agricultural Policy (CAP). True, things have improved from the days when there were butter mountains you could practically ski down, and wine lakes you could metaphorically windsurf across (which were exported at knock-down rates to the Soviet Union), but the cost to the British taxpayer remains exorbitant. It has been estimated that each EU cow has been receiving a subsidy of $2.20 a day. Half the world's population survives on less.

Britain's net contribution to the EU budget, at the last check, was £4.3 billion a year, though this jumps around erratically and will obviously go up by at least a billion following the latest Budget negotiations. About 45 per cent of the EU budget is allocated to the CAP, which means that £1,935 million of our net contribution goes to subsidising farmers in other European countries, including £88 million for tobacco farmers.

In addition to this subsidy, British families on average pay an extra £16 a week for the CAP, because on top of the subsidies paid to farmers and administrators, the price of produce is more expensive at the tills than it otherwise would be.

Big farmers – the so-called 'East Anglia grain barons' – get a good deal. Subsistence farmers do not.

Among the recipients that love the arrangement are the big agrifood companies. Tate and Lyle, for instance, received £127 million in CAP subsidies over 2003-04. That's not what the CAP was set up for.

The Common Fisheries Policy

Then there's the other EU crazy scheme, the Common Fisheries Policy. Cynics like to point out that this was set up as a trap when the Brits, Danes and Irish joined the EEC in 1973, so that the continental fishermen could access our traditional fishing waters. But then, cynics aren't necessarily wrong. The Norwegians voted against joining when their fisheries minister blew the gaffe on the sell-out and resigned.

The problems escalated in the 1980s when the mega fleets of the Spanish and Portuguese were added to the equation. Now, the North Sea is overtrawled; the sand eels that form the basis of the food chain have been overdredged to make cattle feed; and while British boats and crews have been broken up, the Spanish fleet has been receiving masses of EU aid (part funded by the British taxpayer) to upgrade their ports and trawlers.

The crazy quota system means that fishermen have to throw back fish they have caught, which then die as their flotation bladders have exploded, sink to the bottom and pollute the sea bed. The latest figures available, for 2003, show that in Scotland for instance, fishermen were dumping one cod in eight, one haddock in three, and every other whiting. These could have been landed instead and saved both the taxpayers' subsidy and indeed the very livelihood of the trawlermen.

The system is downright pernicious. And it has destroyed the industry. In the 1960s, there were 140 fishing vessels in Fleetwood. Today there are just five.

Were Britain to regain exclusive access to our waters, our fishermen would be able to manage the resources of the home waters responsibly. In time, they would no longer need their current £110 million a year subsidy.

HM Treasury

Factoids

Annual expenditure: £5.31 billion (2005-06)

Administration costs: £4,980 million (2005-06)

Staff: 117,910 [1990: 96,062]

- The Treasury's building at 1 Horse Guards Road, Whitehall, has an estimated value of over £92 million.

- The Treasury spends £750,000 on Special Advisers each year.

- £185,000 is the annual salary of the top civil servant who looks after our money.

- Three silver ink stands that form part of the Treasury's extensive silver collection are worth £200,000 each.

- 87,250 civil servants work for the Inland Revenue.

- 1,400,000,000 coins were minted last year, at a cost of £13.7 million. An unknown number are already behind your sofa.

Gordon Brown is said to be a man of frugal tastes. The Chancellor has made great play of turning down a Jaguar for a cheaper official car. (Perhaps Prescott pinched it?)

It follows, therefore, that the Treasury officials who spend their time telling counterparts across Whitehall to trim their sails must themselves be exemplars of fiscal prudence and rectitude. Of all bureaucrats, they, surely, can be counted upon to spend taxpayers' money wisely?

Erm, no.

Take the saga of **Gordon's dog**. The Treasury hired a small brown dog for a television advertisement publicising tax credits. The dog was required to 'steal' a letter and bury it in the garden. When Gordon Brown saw the advert he said, "I want a labrador in the advert".

The remake cost taxpayers £20,000.

Or there's the case of the **Child Trust Fund** (also known as Baby Bonds). These are issued automatically, but £5 million was wasted on advertising. This was just before the 2005 election. Strange that.

In 2003-04, a staggering £308 million was spent by the Government on **advertising and public relations.** There was a time when the state happily contented itself with instructing citizens to clunk click before every trip, or (if you remember the 1970s advert) warning that if you loitered in a box junction an enormous hand would come down and pick you up. Now, it shamelessly squanders massive amounts of your money telling you how it is spending even more massive amounts of your money, and hinting that you should be grateful.

This basic self-publicising rule does not apply, however, to the Treasury's own involvement in the Euro debate. The Government remains committed, officially at least, to joining the Euro when five conditions (drawn up on the back of a fag packet in a taxi) have been met. Notwithstanding a longstanding argument within Government on whether these five tests would ever be met, the Government resolved to start preparing itself just in case it did decide at some point to ditch the Pound.

By close of March 2004, the total spend on public sector Euro preparations had run to £43 million. Of this, £20 million had been forked out by the Inland Revenue, £8.8 million by HM Customs and Excise, and £9.7 million by the Department for Work and Pensions. All this, before Parliament had even voted, and before a promised referendum had been held – let alone won – for a decision that will probably never be made.

Then there was the 1999 fiasco of the Chancellor selling off half of the **British gold reserves**, just when the price had hit rock bottom in a 20 year slump. The price obtained for the 415 tonnes was around $260 per ounce. Since then, it has risen inexorably to its current high of $540.

One of the reasons the price achieved was so low was that the Bank of England made the basic error of announcing its intention to sell the country's gold in advance, and told the market exactly how much and when it would be holding the series of auctions. Traders in the market couldn't believe their luck. As a way of ensuring that taxpayers got the worst possible price, the Old Lady couldn't have done better (worse).

Except in one respect – the auction rules. The rules set by the Bank actually mitigated against getting a full price. Below is the

Bank's statement in May 1999 on how the price would be set:

> *"The first auction will be conducted on a single, or uniform, price basis. Under this format, the bidding process will be competitive: bars will be allotted to the highest bidders, but all successful bidders will pay a single price that is equal to the lowest accepted bid."*

The key bit is the last line. Translated, it means that the gold would be sold to the highest bidders *not at the price they bid*, but at the price equal to the *lowest accepted bid*. As one incredulous American expert put it:

> *"This goofy Dutch Auction process is fine for bidding on beanie babies and other fungible junk on E-Bay, but is it proper when liquidating 58% of the public gold of one of the greatest western nations in history? Why use an auction process that ensures that Her Majesty's Treasury receives the lowest price possible for valuable gold?"*

To add insult to injury, the British taxpayer, through the good offices of the Treasury, had to fork out compensation to Third World gold mining countries on the grounds that Britain had, by flooding the market, caused them losses.

Part of the problem is training – or lack of it. The Treasury does not have any requirement for its Finance Directors to be qualified accountants, or even to have equivalent skills and a proven track record. In January 2004 only 39 per cent of the Treasury's Finance Directors were qualified accountants – compared to at least 84 per cent of FTSE 100 companies.

David James, the company troubleshooter best known for salvaging the Millennium Dome on behalf of the Government, describes the Treasury's civil servants as "the thickest bunch of civil servants I have ever come across". When asked if he would consider relocating Treasury staff whose presence in London was not vital, he replied: "They are all non-vital staff at the Treasury."

"The government that robs Peter to pay Paul can always depend upon the support of Paul."

George Bernard Shaw

Department for Work and Pensions

Factoids

Annual expenditure: £8.62 billion (2005-06) excluding benefits

Administration costs: £6,019 million (2005-06)

Staff: 145,680 [1990: 129,028]

- The DWP spent £370 million in 2004 hiring 5,930 consultants.

- £6.3 million in winter fuel allowance was paid out in the period 2002-03 to pensioners living in Spain.

- £7,000 was claimed by a benefits cheat who claimed to be a single mother whilst living with her husband. She was only exposed after appearing in the TV show *Wife Swap*.

- According to the Government's 2004 *Gershon Review*, 30,000 of the DWP's civil servants are expendable and should go. By December 2005, no one had yet been sacked.

- The Health and Safety Executive employs 4,080 people. Like the Food Standards Agency (workforce: 670) its work duplicates that of organisations in Brussels, and the quango's main *raison d'être* is to hide the true origin of health and safety legislation.

Ironically, staff at the Department for Work have one of the highest sickness rates in government. They average 12.6 days a year off – over 50 per cent higher than the rate of the private sector. This costs the taxpayer £100 million a year.

DWP management has come up with an unusual way of addressing its absenteeism problem, copying an initiative pioneered by the Royal Mail. In August 2005, the DWP launched a scheme in which staff who took no sick leave over a six month period could win one of 37 Ford Focus cars. 90,000 other staff would receive a £150 holiday voucher. Attendance levels did rise, though it remains to be seen just how cost effective this bribery for *doing-the-job-you've-already-been-paid-to-do* has been.

The real waste scandals at the DWP are its failing policies, among them the much-trumpeted New Deal.

The New Deal

The New Deal is the Government's flagship policy for getting people off welfare and into work, and what an expensive failure it has turned out to be. In 2002, the National Audit Office found that of the 339,000 18-24 year olds who had supposedly found work through the New Deal for Young People, only 8,000 who would not otherwise have found work had been placed in sustained jobs.

The various New Deal programmes also suffer from huge and wasteful administrative costs. Only one fifth of the New Deal spending allocated for young people in 2002-03 was spent on the young unemployed themselves, and only 18 per cent of the budget for over-25s was spent on the unemployed over 25. The rest went on administration.

Evidence from the New Deal for Lone Parents is similar: 75 per cent of lone parents now in work say they would have found a job without the New Deal and 76 per cent of the spending in 2002-03 went on admin. The combined cost of the New Deal for Young People, the 25 Plus and Lone Parents was £677 million in 2003-04.

Still on the subject of job creation, but this time in Northern Ireland, the Public Accounts Committee damned *Jobskills* as one of the worst-run programmes that the Committee had examined in recent years. They noted an astonishing catalogue of failures and control weaknesses, all of which pointed to a disturbing level of complacency within the Department. From 1995 to March 2003, Jobskills had catered for some 93,000 people at a total cost of £485 million. The evidence suggested, therefore, that the actual unit cost per job created by Jobskills was of the order of £22,000, which the Committee rightly deemed to be rather poor value for money.

Fraud and Error

Fraud and error in the benefits system is an even bigger culprit than barmy job creation schemes, wasting £2.6 billion a year according to a recent National Audit Office report. Labour MP Frank Field believes that the real figure could be as high as £7 billion.

Some measure of the incompetence can be gleaned from the fact that, because of uncertainties in measuring fraud and error, figures have to be rounded to the nearest £500 million! The

DWP is working to improve measurement but some estimates are more than six years old, because priority has been given to the highest risk benefits such as Income Support, Jobseeker's Allowance and Housing Benefit. Even the Department itself calculates that 4.9 per cent of expenditure on these benefits is lost in fraud.

Nothing, however, has happened to suggest that the situation has or will be improved. The DWP was unable to find supporting papers in 106 out of 800 Incapacity Benefit cases selected by the National Audit Office for checking. Without these records, including medical reports, the benefit cannot be administered effectively.

Inadequacies remain in the Department's systems for accounting for 'customers' (i.e. claimants) who have been overpaid and who owe the DWP money, which totalled £1.1 billion in March 2004. There is no satisfactory audit trail.

Of the estimated £9 billion overpaid in the last three years, £550 million has been recovered but the rest is expected to be written off. Four years after the introduction of resource accounting, the Department still does not know how much it is owed by a significant number of its 'customers'.

Around 2,600 staff work in debt recovery, at a cost of £48 million, or 23p per £1 of debt collected.

Things could obviously be improved.

Incapacity Benefit

Unnecessary payment of Incapacity Benefit is a significant problem. Jane Kennedy MP, when Minister for Work in 2004, admitted that a third of the country's 2.7 million Incapacity Benefit claimants could work immediately, and another third could potentially return in the longer term. Only the final third are sick enough to be off work and on benefits for good.

Incapacity Benefit costs taxpayers £12 billion a year. Cutting the number of claimants in line with Jane Kennedy's calculations would save taxpayers £4 billion.

The Department actually budgets more than £475 million a year for **overpayment of benefits** due to errors by officials. In 2002-03, overpayments included £140 million of Income Support, £110 million of Jobseeker's Allowance, £100 million of Housing Benefit, £50 million of Minimum Income Guarantee, £43 million of Incapacity Benefit and Severe Disability Allowance and £14 million of other Long-Term Benefits.

The think tank *Reform* quite rightly states that with £1 in every £8 in the economy spent on benefits, the system is "an open invitation to fraud". They suggest practical improvements such as increasing the number of home visits to check on benefit fraud and making people sign on to receive unemployment benefit every two days. They also correctly highlight that the whole system needs to be totally rewritten. The current systems have destroyed the DWP's credibility.

The Child Support Agency

Dating back to the last Conservative government is the well-publicised disaster of the Child Support Agency. The system it administers collects only £1.86 for every £1 it costs to run – compare that to the Austrians, who collect on a ratio of eight for one. And its computer system may still take another four years to run properly. The Chief Executive still got a gong in the 2004 New Year Honours List though.

Tax Credits

Tax credits are another high-profile fiasco. The Government replaced the Working Families and Disabled Person's Tax credits with the Child Tax Credit and Working Tax Credit (New Tax Credits) in April 2003.

Some 5.7 million families received New Tax Credits during 2003-04 at a cost of around £16 billion. Of these, several hundred thousand claimants were overpaid New Tax Credits, mainly because of the inherent design of the schemes, but also because of software errors. In some cases, the Treasury was sending out letters saying it would continue to pay out for another six months but then would have to reclaim the whole lot!

The fiasco has led to 21,600 compensation payouts over a twelve month period for bad service, and five thousand letters to the department from MPs.

The DWP published figures in June 2005 showing that some 1.8 million (or 33 per cent) of claimants had been overpaid in 2003-04, partly due to the complexity of the scheme. The Department also found that routine housekeeping software incorrectly deleted almost one million taxpayer records in the period 1997 -2000, resulting in over 360,000 unidentifiable taxpayers not receiving repayments due and 22,000 others not paying tax that was due.

The woes of the DWP, and more particularly of the citizens who come into contact with it, are endless. What we see is a triple issue:

In the first place –
Public money is being wasted at a phenomenal rate, and nobody is being held to account.

In the second place –
Those who really need support from the state are not necessarily getting it, because the system is overwhelmed.

In the third place –
Those who do need state support and who get it may be overpaid and their finances thrown into long term disarray when they are obliged to pay it all back.

It makes your blood boil.

Equally grim is the development of a **dependency culture.** The number of Incapacity Benefit claimants has gone up by 116,000 since 1997; one in six of the working age population is now on some sort of benefit; and one third of all households are dependent on the state for more than half their incomes.

Any sane person recognises that the state is not there to provide for those on leave because of minor 'stress' and 'aches and pains'. Certainly not for the comedy types so regularly exposed by the tabloids who get a black belt in martial arts while claiming a disability pension. Spongers like these take their benefits directly from your taxes, and leech from the genuinely needy.

And then there was . . .

- The *Sure Start Plus* scheme allocated up to £232,750 over five years for free beauty treatments and glamour photo shoots for teenage mothers.

- £50,000 allocated by the Inclusion and Cosmopolitan Board for a manager to handle the quango's £20,000 budget.

Department for International Development

Factoids

Annual expenditure: £4.48 billion (2005-06)

Administration costs: £239 million (2005-06)

Staff: 1,820

- The Chief Executive of the Commonwealth Development Corporation, which is managed by DfID, is paid £380,000 per year. Third World employees of the Corporation get as little as £3 a day.

- £15,378.28 was paid by DfID as compensation to an employee working overseas who had stored her British belongings at the Department's expense. Unfortunately, the Department failed to pay the storage company which, quite within its rights, sold her belongings.

- £11,000 was handed over by the Department to the Treasury for getting its national insurance sums wrong.

Of all the Government departments, you'd think that the Department for International Development would be the least susceptible to waste and extravagance. Dealing as they do with the genuinely deprived in poor countries, its staff know how far a Dollar, Pound and Euro can go when spent in the right way.

Well, some of them may do, but the value-for-money meter

seems to be turned off when it comes to employing consultants. In 2003-04, DfID spent £697 million – *more than a fifth of its budget* – on consultants to advise it how to help the poor, rather than on actually helping the poor.

Not that the advice always works. The £1 million aid package to Swaziland was all set for an increase when, in the nick of time, someone pointed out that the King of Swaziland was planning a million pound birthday party, to add to the £9 million he'd recently spent on refurbishing his palaces and expanding his BMW collection.

Furthermore, because of post-colonial angst in certain pipe-smoking circles in the West, real policies and activities that could provide long term improvements in the Third World have often been sidelined in favour of throwing guilt money at a problem. While development aid can literally be a lifesaver, it can also be a prop to tyranny.

Corruption today is still eating up more money than provided for by aid. Take Nigeria. Forty years of development aid has given Africa £220 billion. £220 billion is also, coincidentally, the amount swindled by corrupt politicians in Nigeria, a country which makes up one seventh of Africa's sum population.

According to Oxfam, the administration that goes with the mass of donor agencies actually adds a heavy burden to Third World governments. It has estimated that only 10 per cent gets spent on the really critical areas. Observers note wryly how the European Commission has concentrated its big money on aid to countries on its borders, some of which have or will probably join the EU.

There are cases like the whistleblower who blew the lid on corruption over £18 million of development aid to Ghana's education system. He got sacked. This does nothing to foster good government, and everything to encourage public money going to support bad men.

Aid can also get lost due to incompetence. The British Government flew over 475,000 ration packs to the USA in response to Hurricane Katrina. Some were distributed, until it was noticed that they did not comply with US regulations on the import of processed meat. They fell foul of a ban on mad cow meat countries and the whole lot was junked.

And then there was . . .

- £13 million spent on hiring 35 consultants in Iraq. On average, each one is getting paid twenty times what the ordinary soldiers actually going out on patrol are getting, which works out at about one third of a million each.

- £9 million spent on civil service travel. This is the equivalent of £5,000 per UK-based DfID civil servant. Development charities send their staff economy. DfID personnel, unlike other government departments, can upgrade to first and business class.

Ministry of Defence

Factoids

Annual expenditure: £30.94 billion (2005-06)

Administration costs: £2,873 million (2005-06)

Staff: 94,470

- There are now more MoD civil servants than front-line soldiers.

- £4 billion has been spent on a new MoD computer system to link 70,000 desks worldwide.

- The MoD fell for a massive fraud and paid out £2,500,000 on a battalion of imaginary troops.

- £1 million has been paid in compensation over the last four years to bullied squaddies.

- The MoD recently spent £272,600 on eight paintings "because we didn't want to use second-rate paintings of dead admirals".

- £2,500 was spent to enable an RAF aircraftswoman to retrain as a pole dancer. Stephanie Hulme was flown from her base in Northern Ireland and put up in a London hotel so that she could enrol in the stripping course.

- 6,000 MoD policemen – the Department's private police force – guard the armed forces.

Never let it be said that the TaxPayers' Alliance is a team of bean counters who cannot appreciate a bit of verve. We like to see élan and decent fighting spirit amongst our troops. That's why we aren't going to criticise the pilot of the military helicopter who took his chopper on a jaunt delivering pizza to his girlfriend on an exercise (only to land and blow dust all over the commander of Sandhurst who happened, by rotten bad luck, to be nearby). Or the pilot in Gulf War One rumoured to have crashed when buzzing allied tanks while waving a Sooty glove puppet from the cockpit.

No, the TaxPayers' Alliance takes issue with the real waste in the MoD, and that happens in **defence procurement**.

According to National Audit Office figures, the cost of major defence projects went over budget by £2,700 million last year and delivery times were also poor. A leaked MoD report has revealed that the £20 billion Eurofighter jets cannot fly in cloud or engage in aerial combat, which one would think would be useful capabilities for a jetfighter. And the Joint Strike Fighter jets will cost an extra £60 million because they are too heavy. However, for a textbook study of poor procurement the Bowman radio system takes some beating.

The Bowman Radio System

The Bowman Radio System was supposed to be in service back in the early 1990s. Its cost was going to be £1.9 billion, no £2.1 billion, no better make that £2.4 billion, as the overspends rocketed with every report.

Five years after the contract had been re-tendered to a new consortium in 2000, the Director of Infantry was still reportedly said to have told his staff he had been forced to accept it with all its faults "for political reasons".

On some settings, the user was getting radiation burns. The boffins eventually solved the problem by, *erm* . . . ditching those settings and reducing the set's capability.

The set weighs 15lbs, three times the weight of its 1960s predecessor, the Clansman. It is reported to have an inflexible, complex and breakable wiring system, and batteries with a more limited life that are harder to obtain and less hard wearing.

It can't work in anything armoured.

And it breaks Land Rover axles.

Oh, and a store of them overheated and burned down a barracks.

Apart from that it's brilliant.

Where does the fault lie for the botched Bowman Radio project? Well, some of it at least lies with the MoD, which apparently added more capability requirements including extra software after placing the initial order.

Another example of escalating overspend is the **Future Rapid Effects System** (FRES). Costs have soared from £6 billion to £14 billion. The extra money could have bought an entire *rootin' tootin'* aircraft carrier battle group for the Royal Navy instead.

Originally, the plan was to do a joint project with the US, but this was then abandoned to link in with EU partners, clearly for political reasons. It turns out, however, that the non-US technology is second rate, and will be incompatible the next time we find ourselves operating alongside US troops. You wonder who the victims of the next friendly fire incident will be able to sue.

Yet another example: **GCHQ**. The cost of relocating the Government's headquarters for electrospooks has escalated from £1.07 billion to £1.62 billion. This is partly due to the higher building and maintenance costs announced by IAS, the controversial private finance initiative consortium in charge of the building project. Shockingly, however, most of the increase is due to a ten-fold rise to £450 million in the cost of transferring the Department's computer system, of which £43 million is being spent on 200 staff working on the system in the old premises until 2012.

Overall, defence procurement for the main items alone is running at 10 per cent over budget – that's £2.7 billion. The TaxPayers' Alliance calculates that the top 20 items are collectively running at over 31 years late. This doesn't include projects like the Landing Ships Dock (Auxiliary), or, ahem, LSD for short. They were billed at £148 million for the pair, and are currently at £309 million and rising.

The effect of this waste is that, while tax money goes down the drain, our servicemen are not getting the equipment that they need. Two new aircraft carriers have been promised, but with no reliable estimates of their cost and an understandably jittery Treasury, there is still no guarantee that they will enter into service. You only have to look at what happened to the new Nimrod MRA4 to see the dangers: overspend on the Nimrod has led to repeated cutbacks. The initial order was for 21. This got cut to 18. Now it stands at 12. The reasons for wanting 21 in the first place have not gone away. But like the concept of dropping the Eurofighter's cannon to save a couple of million pounds, penny-pinching cuts in at the wrong end of the line.

Similar things are happening in **staffing**. Cutbacks in armed forces numbers have led, not to economies, but to extra expense. Soldiers have to spend more time deployed, and less time being trained or with their families. The strain on relationships can be devastating. In turn, this leads to a high turnover of staff, which means having to spend more money on recruiting and training, or, in the case of certain professionals, more on huge bonuses to keep them. The gaps still have to be filled in the meantime. Agency staff have to be hired. Contract staff like medics who, in both senses of the expression, plug the holes out in Iraq are getting £600 per day.

Neither is the Ministry of Defence immune from the evils of the **compensation culture**.

Soldier, the Army's in-house magazine, has revealed that the MoD's compensation bill comes to £600 million, once the costs of investigating claims, lost man-days, recruiting and training new staff, and replacing equipment are included. Official figures show that compensation claims have quadrupled over the past ten years.

In one sense there is nothing new here. During the days of the

Cold War when the British Army carried out exercises on the Rhine, there was a tradition of German farmers encouraging soldiers to trash a small area of their fields so they could claim compensation for all of them. There have also been reports of Kenyan prostitutes lodging sexual assault claims as part of the suing spree from that country a couple of years back.

Obviously, there are cases where compensation is fully justified. The Foreign and Commonwealth Office runs a 'Conflict Prevention Fund' that the British army uses in Iraq to compensate people who have suffered loss or injury caused by its personnel. As at 31st March 2005, 1,563 claims on this fund had been made by Iraqi citizens, and £506,328 paid out in damages, the vast majority relating to road accidents and property damage. This is small beer in the general scheme of things. It is also a fair and sensible use of funds, and helps keep the peace.

Other cases are more questionable. The MoD's Annual Report for Compensation reviews compensation payments over the course of each year. The 8th edition begins with this poem.

> *"Each loss has its compensation*
> *There is healing for every pain*
> *But the bird with the broken pinion*
> *Never soars high again"*

Hezekiah Butterworth (1839-1905)

Very soothing.

On the face of the report, the MoD paid out £63.5 million in compensation last year and got back £1.4 million by suing other people. The real deficit is, however, much larger, because there are significant hidden costs, such as 'non-compensation' payments and legal costs which are not included in the £63.5m.

Estimates by the Health and Safety Executive for claims against the MOD in the UK put this figure variably between 8 and 36 times the amount of compensation paid. In their words, "It is clear that the hidden costs of Ministry of Defence incidents, even on the most conservative basis, are huge". Examples of the more interesting reported claims include:

- £200 awarded to the owner of a parrot scared by a jet.

- £51,000 for six service personnel injured falling out of bed.

- £81,000 to four soldiers for badly fitting boots.

- £30,900 to an 80-year-old lady who broke her wrist when blown off her feet by a Chinook helicopter.

- £3,800 to a woman whose superior leapt from behind a pillar during a team-building exercise and rugby tackled her.

- £30,000 when a low-flying helicopter spooked a racehorse.

- £100,000 to someone injured when their car hit a rising bollard as he was leaving a base.

It's not all bad news, though. The MoD got back £57,200 from the driver of a ride-on lawnmower who ploughed into a helicopter.

Office of the Deputy Prime Minister

Factoids

Annual expenditure: £9.22 billion (2005-06)

Administration costs: £287 million (2005-06)

Staff: 5,450

- £80 million was spent in 2004-05 on consultants. £53 million of which went on hiring 102 consultants at an average of half a million pounds each.

- £2 million was given to the ODPM by the EU to send experts over to Eastern Europe to advise them how to prepare for EU subsidies.

- One third of the new homes built in the South East for nurses, teachers and policemen are still empty.

Good old Two Jags. If you are looking for a minister who takes a helicopter out of town while his car drives up after him to collect him, you can depend on the former supremo who simultaneously ran both Transport and the Environment.

One of the ODPM's jobs is to look after the fire service. So ultimately the buck stops here for the £22 million training centre for London firefighters. It caught fire. By all accounts it got quite toasty in there, because it had no smoke detectors and no sprinklers, and was only spotted by an off-duty fireman. As it was badly ventilated it got very hot, causing extensive smoke damage. Sadly, the building had only been finished the previous year, after a cost and time overrun.

Another of Prezza's jobs has been looking after the regions. Part of this has involved the big spend on demolishing and revitalising the North, a project which has unfortunately got completely out of hand. The Government is now buying up Victorian homes worth up to £145,000, still happily occupied by residents, in order to knock them down and build estates. One street worth £3.5 million is being compulsory purchased so they can bulldoze it. The estimated bill for this plank fest in Yorkshire alone is £140 million. In Liverpool, residents are complaining at the seemingly random decisions on which areas are for the chop, while whole brown field areas lie derelict. Ringo Starr apparently complained when he found out the home where he was born is going to be levelled.

The problem has been the costings. £1.3 billion was pledged to buy and destroy 400,000 homes. The Department, sadly, timed its announcement just before a mini property boom.

On a positive note, Prescott's people have only spent £3 million on office furniture since 1997. That's positively stingy when you consider that the Cabinet Office has spent £104 million, Work and Pensions £323 million, and Health £104 million.

Unfortunately, they then went and spoiled it by spending nearly fifty grand on potted plants.

Section Three

Other Areas of Waste

In this section we home in on specific areas of waste outside central government. Some of these, like devolved government, are well-publicised sinkholes for taxpayers' money, consuming a great deal and offering little in return.

Others, like local government, are more complex. There are councils that are well run, and which offer excellent value for money. And there are others which are spendthrift, inefficient and, at worst, corrupt.

We also look at the cost of politicians – both national and European. Whilst our elected representatives are woolly-minded in so many things, they are razor sharp when it comes to protecting their own financial interests.

Taxpayers will, perhaps, take most fright at the chapter on the public sector generally. We have already seen how individual departments spend your money. Now, we look at figures for the public sector as a whole – its ballooning numbers, its breathtaking wage bill, and its extravagant pension provision.

Finally, we debunk a popular myth – that the Royal Family costs taxpayers money. Republicans are fond of attacking the monarchy as a "waste of public resources". The truth is that the monarchy is a net contributor to the Treasury, not a drain – in stark contrast to politicians themselves.

Folk Heroes and and Folk Zeros

Many popular folk heroes have earned their legendary status by leading tax rebellions. As readers will recall, Lady Godiva appealed to her husband to reduce Coventry's oppressive taxes. After much wifely nagging, the Count promised the Countess that he would comply with her wish on one condition: she must ride through the town naked – an act which is re-enacted to this day in pageants in Coventry.

Gordon Brown is often wrongly described as the 'Robin Hood Chancellor' for taking money from the rich and giving it to the poor. However, a closer inspection of the legend shows this to be an incorrect analogy. The villains of the tale were Prince John, the head of government, and the Sheriff of Nottingham, in charge of local government and the chief tax collector. Robin Hood took from people who were rich because of the taxes they took from the poor taxpayers of Nottinghamshire. Mr Chancellor, we've read *Robin Hood*, and you're no Robin Hood.

Devolved Government

We've gone up to the Himalayan summit of national spending by Government departments. Now let's turn to another layer of government, the Ben Nevises of local politics.

Scotland seems a fair place to start. The former Labour minister who devised the controversial formula that sees Scotland receive more money per head than the rest of the United Kingdom has called for the system to be scrapped. Lord Barnett believes that the formula that bears his name is unfair and he regards it as an embarrassment. The *Barnett Formula* results in the five million Scots receiving £537 per person more government support than those living in the north of England. This amounts to over £2.68 billion each year.

You don't have to look far to see where a chunk of the money has gone. The cost of the Scottish Parliament building has soared from the £40 million initial estimate, announced by Donald Dewar, the late First Minister in the late 1990s, to £431 million. The vote by Members of the Scottish Parliament to approve the plans was extremely close. Had they been aware that consultants for the Scottish Parliament already expected costs to be £88 million, the project may not have gone ahead. Intriguingly, the management did such a marvellous job of chucking money down the drain that if they rebuilt it tomorrow to exactly the same specification, it would still cost £80 million less.

The site was originally a brewery, so the expression about being incapable of organising a function at one is witheringly apt.

Surprise, surprise, other devolved forms of government show exactly the same free-spending tendency. The estimated cost of the Welsh Assembly together with the Wales Office was £92 million, but in 2002-03 the figure increased to £177 million.

Similarly, the annual running costs for the Greater London Authority have trebled to £60 million a year, from a projected figure of £20 million in 1998. Combined, the Welsh Assembly and the GLA are therefore over budget by £125 million a year.

In the North, meanwhile, John Prescott has wasted at least £30 million in his failed attempt to set up elected Regional Assemblies, a move decisively stopped when the North East voted four to one against the proposals, a reflection of people's natural scepticism of politicians.

This is in addition to the £18 million cost of the eight existing unelected Regional Assemblies and the £124 million running costs for the Government Offices of the Regions. It's a level of government nobody wants, with the power to do pretty well nothing, at a cost nobody has voted to pay.

Newcastle City Council allows rent-free occupation for the North East Assembly, when it could hire out the space for £200,000. That, however, would make the Assembly look like a direct drain on the taxpayer. In comparison, the South Eastern Assembly Council delegates voted by a two thirds majority to scrap it as a waste of money – but were legally unable to do so.

Then there is London. Residents there are starting at last to remember why Red Ken was so controversial in the 80s. First there was the introduction of the Congestion Charge. Then the charge went up from £5 to £8, supposedly to pay for public transport. Then bus and tube fares were put up by 20 per cent regardless.

The signs are ominous. The budget of the GLA has gone up by a fifth in four years, to almost £3 billion – a detail few people appear to have noticed. Our Ken's personal office now costs £13.9 million to run. The 250 GLA staff have rapidly expanded to 682. Even the City Hall building cost £43 million, with structural flaws now reported because of the increased weight of personnel!

Ken has 58 media and marketing officers on the payroll. Six of his advisers are on six figure salaries. He has blown £1.1 million funding the European Social Forum for Marxists and Anarchists. He's thrown away another £1.1 million in legal fees against the Government over who runs the Tube. And we haven't even started on the cost of him engaging in a whole series of politically correct activities, including membership of the Association of Nuclear Free Authorities.

But then, this is the same team which has had to fork out to replace the plaque on a controversial statue in Trafalgar Square, because they spelt 'resilience' wrong.

The Top 5 Places a Politician has Represented his Constituents From*

1.   Prison

2.   His new home in Germany

3.   Glasgow (representing Lewisham)

4.   The West Country (representing Bromley)

Those were Councillors. Then there was:

5.   Northern Ireland (as an MP)

Over the period 2001-03, Sinn Fein claimed £827,000 in office, staffing and travel subsidies without taking their seats, and a reported £472,485 during 2004-05. They also claimed £15,000 for second homes in London.

*and *still* got his allowance

Local Government

From the foothills of regional government, we continue our trek down to the flood plains that are those bits of government nearest to taxpayers.

Sadly, this is precisely the area which furnishes so many of the waste and fraud stories that end up in the pages of the supreme waste-watcher, *Private Eye*. Perhaps if you hold office in an area that hasn't changed political colour in 80 years, the temptation to treat it like a personal fiefdom is simply too great. Or maybe power goes to some people's heads too easily. Whatever the reason, personal gain and favour are a perennial feature of local politics.

Central government subsidies on the scale of the £2 billion *New Deal for Communities* play into the hands of those who would abuse the system. The ten year scheme was established to fund the regeneration of inner cities, with 39 local boards distributing £53 million of taxpayers' money apiece. It has been branded a flop after increasing evidence of gross mismanagement and waste.

Just one example: Aston Pride, serving north Birmingham, was disbanded in 2003 for failing to follow basic rules such as setting up a bank account or obtaining a cheque book, which even students on their first day of university can sort out. Yet it managed to spend nearly £2.4 million on administration.

Overall, £257 million was allocated to the New Deal last year, of which nearly £22 million was spent on management and administration.

It comes as no surprise that there is waste in the public library system, but the *level* of waste may come as a shock. A report by the charity *Libri* estimates that as much as a fifth of the £1 billion national library budget is wasted every year on over-elaborate management, inappropriate use of staff, outmoded practices, unnecessary administration and general inefficiency. Every library visit now costs £3 and libraries spend £24 every time they buy a £10 book.

Local government, even more than cental government, is on the sharp end of bogus and excessive compensation claims. A report commissioned for the insurance firm Norwich Union found that claims against local councils have reached £117 million a year. For example, minor compensation claims for "trips and slips" cost Manchester City Council over £2 million in 2003. What is Deansgate, an assault course?

The root cause of the problem is the mentality of a lot of the lawyers and some of the claimants. Consider the case of the two housing benefit claimants who found £24,550 in their bank account. Thinking Christmas had come early, they lived the high life, lavished themselves with electrical goods and holidays abroad, and ignored repeated pleas from Derby City Council to return the money given to them in error. They were later jailed for six months for theft. *Neighbours* then pinched the plot.

Worse, according to the CBI, councils are wasting at least £3 billion a year because they are inept at squeezing value out of private sector contractors. "Local government does not appear to be making the best use of competition. This is because of two barriers: a lack of commitment and a lack of procurement skills."

A classic recent example was the move to rebrand Nottinghamshire. Already the council had excitement on a stick, with an internationally recognised brand in Robin Hood. But no, Notts tourism bosses had to play the Sheriff and spend tax money hiring a PR firm for an image revamp. After two years of thinking, they dumped the Robin Hood logo in favour of a chunky 'N'. Cost to the taxpayer: £120,000.

A trendy £400 Birmingham City Council project to paper a subway with pop art survived a few hours before environmental health officials from another council department cleaned them all off. The artist, who spent nine hours pasting the photocopied designs on to the walls, described the council officials as being "as daft as a brush".

Some of the contracting work, meanwhile, is taken to Soviet era levels of employment. Officials at Hull City Council told a councillor that it costs £50 to change a 35p light bulb. Council workers must report the blown bulb to superintendents, who then send a fax to the property services department, who finally send out an electrician. Or four electricians, if they abide by health and safety rules and electrical safety legislation to the letter. According to the head of community care at Doncaster Council, changing a light bulb for an elderly resident requires one person to replace the bulb, another to hold the ladder, a third person to switch off the electricity at the mains and a fourth person to comfort the elderly resident until the operation is completed. There, there.

Another example of how taxpayers' money could be more efficiently used lies in the whole spending structure of local government. In many cases, there is a rigid mechanism for local managers to buy centrally-managed stock. What this means, however, is that there is no freedom to buy cheaper. Up to 25 per cent of the costs are lost simply in paperwork. You thus have cases reported where cans of beans are bought at 80p a tin when the same tin is available for 20p at the local Co-op, and schools forking out hundreds of pounds over the odds to get their computers. Frank Doran, former Mayor of Liverpool, calls it "a complete waste of money".

Bath Council deserves extra credit. It's behind the building of a new spa, which ran out of water. A borehole missed its target and had to be redrilled. A second one also failed. The cost so far is £33 million, a mixture of council tax and lottery money. It's three years behind schedule and three times over estimate, costing local taxpayers £98 each.

It would be cheaper to deliver a bath of Perrier water to every household.

Vandals then smashed the £180,000 exposed glass panels in front of the building. In August 2003, Domingo, Carreras and Pavarotti were flown in for an opening concert, but this was impossible due to the discovery of flakey paint in the swimming pool.

In Deadman's Gulch you might expect this. But this in a town with so much water it's actually called Bath, for Pete's sake.

A Call to Arms

The examples of waste in this book are based on reported facts and stories in the public domain. We believe that many more billions of waste are hidden away in the growing Leviathan of our state sector.

The TPA has launched its **WasteWatchers 2006** campaign as a way for taxpayers to report public sector waste and useless spending. We have already gathered lots of new material for next year's edition of *The Bumper Book of Government Waste* and welcome further suggestions.

If you have come across examples of waste where you live, please let us know. By now, you'll know the sort of thing we're looking for:

- £1.4 million on a parks police unit given 3 weeks training but no actual powers.

- £170,000 spent flying 120 head teachers and councillors to the USA to visit schools.

- £16,560 on a town-twinning trip for councillors to Johannesburg (excluding the safari trip which was subsequently repaid).

- £15,000 spent on a bronze statue of dinosaur dung for a village.

Send us an email at info@taxpayersalliance.com, or contact us by phone on 0845 330 9554, and ask for 'WasteWatchers'.

Information Technology

Computers. The mainstay of developed society, intragovernmental communications and Western capitalism. Also known as expensive paperweights.

The bill for recent and ongoing government computer projects is estimated at £30 billion. This is known officially in the trade as "a lot of money".

Yet according to the Public Accounts Committee, one in three projects is not checked properly for budget and systems failures. There should be a 'gateway review' to stop deadlines being missed and plans running over budget.

The result of mismanagement is that cancelled or over budget government IT projects cost taxpayers billions of pounds each year. Two flagrant examples are the £67 million *Individual Learning Accounts* IT system which was cancelled in 2004 amid accusations of fraud, and the £450 million *Child Support Agency* computer system which went over budget by £50 million and has caused untold distress to parents ensnared in its web.

The House of Commons Work and Pensions Committee verdict is damning:

> *"Expenditure on IT in the UK public sector in 2003/04 has been estimated to be in excess of £12,400 million, with a significant proportion at risk of being wasted."*

Assuming just ten per cent is wasteful, savings of £1.24 billion are available. But this may be a conservative estimate.

According to *Computer Weekly*, the UK currently spends more on public sector IT than any other country in Western Europe, and almost double that of second-placed Germany.

More than £1.5 billion has been spent on e-Government websites that do not resolve customer queries, according to research published by software company Transversal. The study shows that 60 per cent of government websites are inefficient at resolving customer queries and 75 per cent of customer-related management projects fail to deliver any measurable return on investment. Assuming just a quarter of this money was wasted there are potential savings of £375 million.

An in-depth investigation by the *Guardian* reported that one government website – www.ukworldheritage.org.uk – received only 77 hits last year. By freaky coincidence, two of them were from one of the authors of this book looking for places to go on holiday. He visited a second time because he had forgotten what he had read. The total cost of running this and just ten other linked sites ran to £43 million. And there are now more than 2,500 government websites.

Then there was Transport Direct. This was the £50 million public transport journey planner that came out two years behind schedule, and which recommended, among other things, that travellers should wait at station platforms for six hours rather than taking a 40 minute bus ride. Other recommendations included suggestions that travellers should take picturesque routes by ignoring ferries. In some cases it suggested that you should forget public transport and just take the car.

With such a poor track record, the ID cards project is a terrifying prospect. The Government refuses to say how much it thinks it will cost. One official estimate reportedly came in at £3.1 billion, which then got upgraded to £5.8 billion. Figures from the London School of Economics suggest it could cost £18 billion – in other words we would all have to pay £300 per card.

But even this doesn't take into account the cost of all the monitoring technology, plus the bill for updating the information on the card which will probably need to be done much sooner than the supposed ten year lifespan of the card. On top of that, there's the cost of dealing with people who refuse to carry the card. New technology and staff training is assessed to come to another £10 billion, or an additional £100 to your council tax bill for ten years.

This is not bloody-minded pessimism, as the abysmal history of IT projects in the NHS has shown. The Department of Health has admitted that the NHS National Programme for IT (NPfIT) will cost up to five times the previously stated cost of £6.3 billion over ten years, meaning the total bill could be as high as £30 billion. But it doesn't stop there. According to *Computer Weekly*, an NPfIT official told a private meeting that the cost could hit an enormous £50 billion.

The difference between the two figures is about the same as the total amount of African national debt written off after Live8.

Even if the Government does manage to contain the cost to £30 billion, this still implies an overspend of £2.38 billion a year for ten years. A leaked email from within the Department of Health shows how easily the project could come unstuck. It stated that delays in just one part of the system, a £20 million packet, would not just destabilise but actually *derail* the whole project.

Yet another example that illustrates the government's total inability to procure and run IT projects efficiently: the *e-Bookings* hospital reservation system. The managers of this £196 million white elephant knew they were having problems when the statistics revealed that the booking system had been used a mere 63 times. GPs complained that they found it burdensome to use, so an extra £95 million was pumped in to improve it. Even now, only one in six GPs uses the new, revised system, and they still tend to phone up and check that the booking has been recorded successfully, which rather defeats the whole point.

The danger with government IT is always that the whole system will go completely doolally. Just like the Passports Agency computer system, where 400,000 forms went AWOL.

Politicians

Our political representatives in Parliament are not the most popular of figures. All the sleaze stories from the 90s have left them tarred with a reputation as philandering, crocodile-tear, snake-oil, moolah merchants, who are only marginally less repugnant than estate agents.

This is unfair for two reasons. Firstly, a majority of them are decent, conscientious, hard-working people who have entered politics in order to provide a service to their community and improve the world around them. Secondly, the bad apples keep brown envelope manufacturers in business.

So, how much do politicians cost the taxpayer? Let's start with the direct costs of Members of Parliament:

MPs

Members' Parliamentary Salary	£57,485
Staffing Allowance	£66,458 – £77,534
Incidental Expenses Provision (IEP)	£19,325
IT equipment (centrally provided)	£3,000 (approx)
London Supplement	£1,618
Additional Costs Allowance	£20,902
Car Mileage	up to 57.7p per mile
Motorcycle Allowance	24p per mile
Bicycle Allowance	20p per mile
Winding-Up Allowance	£32,286 (maximum)

plus

- Up to three annual journeys to the European Parliament or another national parliament.

- 30 single trips to and from London for their spouse and each of their children.

- There are also reports of a fridge allowance, and of a £400 food allowance.

In the list on the previous page, you will see that some of the items are variable. It's up to individual MPs to claim back from the public purse expenses they have incurred in doing their job, and the claims they make vary considerably. Some of the higher profile MPs get more 'green ink letters' from crazed constituents than others, so have more post to deal with. But don't think that someone who spends large sums of public money firing off letters is good value for money, because there are all sorts of questionable practices going on, ranging from the dubious and costly norm of sending hundreds of key constituents Christmas cards, to the downright illegal practice of sending out party political propaganda.

Fortunately, information about MPs' expenses is in the public domain, so it's easy to draw up a list of the MPs who cost us the most. Opposite are the names, constituencies and amounts claimed by the top ten spenders of 2005 – which, out of interest, you may remember was an election year.

If it's any consolation, some of them have lost their seats and have sunk once more into the Lethe, never to be seen or spent on again.

Biggest spending MPs for 2005

MP	Constituency	Expenses
Geraint Davies (Lab)	Croydon Central	£176,026
Margaret Moran (Lab)	Luton South	£168,569
Angus Robertson (SNP)	Moray	£160,776
Ashok Kumar (Lab)	Middlesboro' South & East Cleveland	£158,844
Peter Duncan (Con)	Galloway and Upper Nithsdale	£158,032
Lorna Fitzsimons (Lab)	Rochdale	£156,359
Frank Doran (Lab)	Aberdeen Central	£155,696
Mohammad Sarwar (Lab)	Glasgow, Govan	£155,107
Eric Joyce (Lab)	Falkirk West	£155,055
Alan Milburn (Lab)	Darlington	£154,139

Thirteen of the top twenty spenders in the letter allowance league happened to be Labour MPs fighting marginals. The top spender blew £38,750 on postage alone!

Another, less obvious, cost to the taxpayer incurred by MPs is the misuse of Parliamentary Questions (PQs). MPs can hold government ministers to account by writing a PQ and requiring the department's civil servants to come up with answers. But twice now, in the run up to a general election, Labour MPs have submitted questions asking the government's civil servants to say how fantastic they've been. Strangely, these questions have been identical:

"If the minister will set out, with statistical evidence relating as closely as possible to [constituency name], the effects of his Department's policies since 1997."

Ignore the curious phrasing and the lack of a question mark. It *is* a question – well, an invitation, really – phrased according to Parliamentary tradition.

You won't be very surprised to hear that ministers have always been delighted to provide uncharacteristically full replies to these PQs, setting out Government-researched statistics that the MP can use in his election material. A short study of several of these constituencies showed that the replies were totally one-sided, and missed out unfavourable facts such as closed police stations and cutbacks in services. Some Labour MPs even asked questions (against convention) about the constituencies of leading Opposition members who were defending small majorities.

Clearly, this was a wheeze devised by Labour whips for their backbenchers to make political advantage out of the system. The cost limit for each PQ is normally around £200 in terms of civil service time. These PQs would undoubtedly have exceeded that limit, but even if roughly costed on the £200 basis, the total for these 140 questions comes to approaching £30,000. Of course, the cost of abusing the democratic system is higher than that.

Sadly, this behaviour fits into a broader pattern. Government spending on advertising has rocketed to £203 million a year – £144 million more than was spent in 1997. Figures compiled from official departmental statistics show that the Government is now Britain's biggest advertiser, with Procter & Gamble in second place spending £187 million in 2004. But government does not exist to sell a product, especially not if that product is itself.

More money could be saved by ditching postal voting in European and local elections. The Electoral Commission condemned the £21 million all-postal voting in the 2004 local and European elections as a failure and called for an immediate halt to all-postal ballots. Their report highlighted a litany of problems, including claims of electoral fraud, which have damaged public confidence in the electoral system. In any case, it is far better to encourage people to go in person and ponder their vote.

Liberal Democrat MP Andrew George is seeking to cut the number of MPs to 500, saving taxpayers up to £60 million a year. His comparison is one of efficiency cutbacks in private business. The TaxPayers' Alliance fully supports this policy. Perhaps we could start with his colleague, the former Lib Dem Work and Pensions spokesman. He was reportedly claiming £545 in tax credits (a system designed to help the poor). Or Lib Dem MEP Chris Davies, who, in a crudely contrived stunt deliberately got himself arrested in possession of an £8 block of cannabis outside a police station. This wasted 100 hours of police time and cost taxpayers £10,000.

The Parliamentary Estate itself soaks up funds. Expenditure on flowers in the catering outlets of the House of Commons has risen from £7,497 five years ago to £11,513 last year. This bill excludes the flowers on more public display elsewhere in the Palace, which doubles it, and presumably excludes staff costs.

25,000 units of bottled water were used last year, at a cost of £11,505. Yes, there are taps in the Commons.

A few years ago, the building scandal was the expense of Portcullis House. Lessons have not been learnt. Even now, they are spending £422,000 to build a short, covered walkway.

Cabinet Ministers

If you are a minister as well as an MP, you are holding down two jobs and your pay is boosted accordingly.

Prime Minister	£178,922
Cabinet Minister	£130,347
Minister of State	£95,281
Government Chief Whip	£130,347
Government Whip	£81,809
Leader of the Opposition	£124,277
Opposition Chief Whip	£95,281
Speaker	£130,347

On top of their MP benefits, ministers get three months severance pay. This is a cash pay-off worth about £37,000 for a junior minister. It is not clear if Blunkett and Mandelson – double ejectees from the Cabinet – claimed it twice.

Former Prime Ministers are granted a £77,534 allowance to run their office, and an immediate pension of £62,400. So we can expect a Blair Foundation for the Third Way in the near future.

Some ministers have also taken liberties with taxpayers' money by claiming a second homes allowance. Tony Blair has received £16,417 despite having a Downing Street flat. David Blunkett has reportedly been given £20,608, Jack Straw £17,780, John Prescott £14,166, and Margaret Beckett £19,088, despite each of them having grace and favour accommodation.

Margaret Beckett was given rent-free use of a flat in Admiralty Arch, despite not being a security risk, a perk worth an estimated £200,000 per year. Prescott has a country mansion in Dorneywood worth £400,000 in rent, while other flats in Admiralty Arch for other ministers are estimated to be worth a total of £300,000 in rent value per year. Blunkett stayed on in his £1.5 million official Belgravia house even after his first resignation. On top of that, taxpayers also cover the council tax bills for these properties.

National Assembly for Wales Salaries: 2004–05

Assembly First Minister	£116,146
Assembly Minister	£81,080
Presiding Officer	£81,080
Leader of the largest non-cabinet party	£81,080
Chairs of Subject Committees	£48,790
Assembly Member	£43,283

In case you were wondering who looks after them, the Welsh National Assembly employs 4,200 people.

Scottish Parliament Salaries: 2004-05

First Minister	£123,162
Presiding Officer	£88,098
Scottish Minister	£88,098
MSP	£50,300

You may be surprised to learn that MSPs are amongst the most fastidious watchdogs of their personal pockets. Here are some examples of the penny-pinching claims recently put in by our finest Scots representatives, as reported by *The Scotsman*.

MSP	*Claim*	*Amount*
Kate McLean	Office supplies	7p
Brian Monteith	Bridge tolls	13p
Des McNulty	Bus ticket	40p
Jim Mather	Parking ticket	50p
David McLetchie	Newspaper	60p
Rosie Kane	Phone calls	80p
Gordon Jackson	Train ticket	£1.15

Your first thought might be that these are the worthy acts of a responsible bookkeeper. Most of us, however, would take a loss of this size on the chin and recognise that the cost of processing the claims outweighs the personal cost of not claiming.

At the TaxPayers' Alliance, we've been scratching our heads over just what 7p in stationery could get you. We calculate that it equates to half a biro, a plain rubber, eleven paperclips, and an almost but not quite upgrade from second to first class stamp.

Northern Ireland MLAs

Stormont has been costing us an estimated £100 million per year, even while it's been suspended. £30 million has been spent on the salaries of the elected, £40 million on running costs.

MLAs	£28,700 (while suspended, down from £41,000)
Expenses & office allowance	£15,000 to £48,000
Payouts to those who lost seats or did not fight in last election	£1.4 million

The House of Lords

The House of Lords operates on a comparative shoestring when compared to the Commons. Many of its members have second jobs, but this is all the more reason why they should be defended against ill thought-out "reforms" from Downing Street. It gives them a knowledge edge and makes them excellent value for money.

Backbench Peers

Subsistence	£64 (day) or £128 (overnight)
Motor mileage Allowance	57.6p per mile up to 20,000 miles 26.6p per mile further
Bicycle Allowance	7.4p per mile
Spouse's expenses	Two return journeys for Parliamentary occasions per year
Office secretarial Allowance	£53.50 per sitting day and for up to 40 additional days per year

Lords Ministers and Paid Office Holders

Ministers' Night Subsistence Allowance	£28,160 for those who maintain a second home in London. Or who claim that their main London pad is only a working retreat.
London Supplement	£1,618
Secretarial Allowance	£4,742
Expenses	Up to 15 return journeys per year for spouse and children under 18.

A busy backbench peer who attends regularly probably costs the taxpayer about a tenth of the cost of an MP sitting two hundred yards away.

The figures on the preceding pages compare with the following top-scale jobs on the public payroll:

Top Public Payroll Salaries

Mayor of London	£132,000
High Court Judge	£155,404
Chief of the Defence Staff	£205,160
Head of the Metropolitan Police	£215,000
Senior Civil Servants (Permanent Secretaries)	£264,250
Governor, Bank of England	£268,137
British Nuclear Fuels, CEO	£635,711
Network Rail, CEO	£919,000
Royal Mail, CEO	£2,700,000

The Donated Asset Reserve

If you are a minister on an official visit overseas, there's a danger that you'll be given a present by your host country. It may be a plastic Eiffel Tower, in which case you can keep it. Or it may be something more significant like the Holy Lead Piping of Antioch, in which case it belongs to the state. The limit is £140 in value, which can get you a decent ticket to a play but not the whole theatre. It exists to stop the minister saying: "Why thank you for this totally unexpected gift of a Porsche and yes, we will support your country's accession to the EU."

The expensive gifts are handed over to a pool known as the Donated Asset Reserve (which also includes financial bequests to the state by deluded patriots). Since the taxpayer owns these items, we thought you'd like a review of some of the gifts you have received since 2001. Not that you'll ever get to see them.

- When he was Secretary of State for Defence, Geoff Hoon was sent a hamper by the Kuwaiti Ambassador. He took out £140 worth of goodies and handed the rest over.

- The MoD has a Malaysian ornamental kite in a presentation box.

- The FCO was given two Pakistani rugs and a pearl necklace from the wife of the Sheikh of Abu Dhabi.

- The Department of Health has a Reuge 36 music box.

- The Treasury has a T-mobile MDA II pocket PC/mobile phone from the Germans.

As for the Prime Minister's office, it is currently looking after the following for you:

- A Segway Transporter
- Watches
- Sundry vases, porcelain and sculptures
- A book from the French
- A musical box and gold coins
- Two daggers
- 'Israeli archaeological artifacts'
- An electric Ferrari
- A stock of vino collapso
- A nativity scene from Yasser Arafat
- And a "bronze fox" from the Government of Belgium
- Not forgetting the fondu set and the cuddly toy

Didn't he do well?

The prize for the most bizarre gift goes to the Italians, who gave the PM a bracelet, a necklace, some earrings and a ring. Do they know something we don't?

Valéry Marie René
    Georges Giscard d'Estaing
Former President of France
c/o French Embassy
58 Knightsbridge
London SW1X 7JT
December 2005

Dear President d'Estaing,

We understand from our research that during your time as President of the French Republic you were a close friend of Jean-Bédel Bokassa and that you supplied the Central African Republic with considerable financial and military backing. It has also come to our attention that you accepted diamonds as personal gifts from Bokassa and accepted him in France when he fled to your country with looted millions from the Central African Republic's treasury.

We are currently compiling a Bumper Book of Government Waste and we were wondering whether you would be willing to send us your comments on the following point: When you received the diamonds, did you ever consider selling them, giving the money to the French Treasury and reducing the tax burden on hard-working French families?

Thank you in anticipation of your help.

Yours sincerely,

Matthew Elliott
TPA Chief Executive

"For which of you, intending to build a tower, does not sit down first and count the cost, whether he has enough to finish it. Lest, after he has laid the foundation, and is not able to finish, all who see it begin to mock him, saying, 'This man began to build and was not able to finish'."

Luke 14:28-30

The Public Sector

Money slips through public sector fingers in so many ways.

Quangos

There used to be a time when people thought quango was an exotic fruit drink made from the produce of the Opuntia galapageia bush, or a Mexican bandido famed for the 1912 Moustache Raid on the Third National Bank in Puerto Desperado.

All that has changed, and the word has entered public consciousness in a villainous role. Quangos may not be talked about so much now by the Government, because of their connotation with incompetence and waste, but they are still very much part of the state apparatus in the form of over 800 'Public Bodies' and 'Task Forces' created in recent years.

Quangoland costs over £22 billion a year – the equivalent of an extra 5p on the basic rate of income tax – and covers everything from the Active Communities Unit (£84 million) to the Zoos Forum (£35,000).

John Reid appeared to lead the way in tackling quangoland by promising to halve the number of NHS quangos and thereby save £500 million. If the same principle were applied to all quangos, taxpayers could save £11.37 billion a year.

Public Sector Fraud

Public sector fraud cost taxpayers over £83 million in 2002, according to an Audit Commission report on the National Fraud Initiative. The figure has probably increased since – detected public sector crime has risen by 65 per cent since 2001 – but £83 million is the latest figure available.

Overspends

A great deal of taxpayers' money goes down the drain through the inability of Government departments to balance their books. A staggering 20 out of 24 departments overspent their budgets for 2004-05. This racked up a total overspend of £7.1 billion. The Deputy PM alone overshot by £1.6 billion.

Perhaps we should look on the bright side and muse on what could be clawed back. The Government has already raised money by selling public assets such as the National Air Traffic Control Service (£750 million) and the Defence Evaluation and Research Agency (£250 million).

The Liberal Democrats have proposed selling off the Royal Mint, which would provide the taxpayer with an estimated windfall of £200 million. Bisham Abbey – the England football team's training camp in Berkshire owned by the state – could be sold for another £8 million.

Public Sector Jobs

The real root of the problem in public waste comes from the non-jobs, the absenteeism and the generous pensions that bedeck the entire public sector workforce.

The TaxPayers' Alliance has calculated that the annual salary bill for all the jobs advertised in *Guardian Society* in 2005 was a staggering:

$$\boxed{£787,319,556.31}$$

Whatever happened to the Government's commitment to the cost-cutting Gershon Review, and Gordon Brown's promise in his March 2005 Budget to cut tens of thousands of people from the public sector payroll?

The increase in public spending has led to an increase in big money for top jobs. Over 2004-05, the best paid public sector workers received average pay increases of 13 per cent – more than five times the rate of inflation, and three times the rate of their peers in the private sector. Across the public sector as a whole, earnings rose by 4.7 per cent compared with 3.7 per cent in the private workforce.

According to the Office of National Statistics, the average public sector worker now gets paid more than his private sector counterpart. As of 2005, full-time public sector staff took home £475.10 a week on average, £62 more than their counterparts in the private sector.

The average salary for all the jobs advertised in *Guardian Society* in 2005 was £35,509 – a staggering £9,995 more than the mean private sector wage last year. And they still have the old perks of earlier retirement, a final salary pension, and the possibility of a gong to boot.

Average earnings for directors of major public bodies is now around the £170,000 mark. The boss of an average Government agency can expect £100,000 and local authority Chief Executives around £112,000. It's not difficult to spot where the people who run the council estates live – in the posh, leafy patch on the other side of town.

Yet these hikes have rarely been matched by improvements in productivity. With some exceptions (notably front-line staff), public sector workers have greater job security, less pressure, and indeed less responsibility than their counterparts working in the genuine marketplace. They do not generate wealth (because they are spending someone else's), and have all too few efficiency checks. NHS Chief Executives have an awkward tendency to hand themselves 20 per cent higher pay awards than nurses. There was a 16 per cent hike for Chief Constables in 2003, despite crime increases.

Meanwhile, the head of the Government's Climate Change quango was given a £50,000 bonus, despite greenhouse gas emissions getting worse not better. DEFRA claimed that, although it funded the Climate Trust, that body made decisions on pay awards independently. The sound of washing hands can often be heard echoing around Whitehall.

On an hour by hour basis, public sector workers have always had a better deal than those in the private sector. That gap is widening. In 2004, the average private sector employee was working 40.5 hours a week; his counterpart in the public sector, 37.6 hours.

Moreover, state sector absenteeism is 50 per cent higher than in the private sector. The Government's own statistics estimate 10.7 days off against 7.8 days.

It is hardly a surprise, therefore, that the cost of bureaucracy is surging. Central government administration costs reached £21.3 billion in 2003-04, an increase of over 40 per cent since 1998-9. During that time, average prices have gone up by roughly 12 per cent. That's a 28-point difference worth over £5.9 billion.

Between 1998 and mid 2003, employment in the public sector surged by more than 500,000 – though the Office of National Statistics (ONS) has yet to produce up-to-date estimates, which will probably add 100,000 to that figure. Many more workers are due to be taken on over the next three years.

Public sector employment has been rising steadily since 1998 following twenty years of consecutive falls. It reached a high of 7.4 million in 1979 and fell to just over 5 million in 1998.

Between 2000 and 2005, almost one in every two new jobs has been created in the public sector. The latest figures from the ONS show that public sector employment has continued to rise faster than private sector employment, and that growth has been faster among administrators rather than front-line staff.

However, the headline figures significantly underestimate the true size of the modern state sector workforce, because they do not count contractors or freelance workers brought in by

Government at comparatively expensive rates, such as agency nurses. Furthermore, the figures don't show the growth of private finance initiative contracts and other forms of off-balance sheet government activity. These are hidden means of pawning off public assets, and taxpayers will be paying for decades to come.

It is therefore hardly surprising that actual productivity in the state sector fell between 1998 and 2001, according to recent ONS estimates. It has undoubtedly continued to fall since then, as reports leaked to *The Sunday Times* have shown.

However, because of the controversial changes pushed through to the way the statistics are calculated for 2004, the official figures may stop showing such declines in productivity in the future. This doesn't mean that they are not taking place. The continued surge in waste proves that the Government's real productivity record remains dismal, regardless of what the official figures may claim.

Until Gordon Brown admits that his tax and spend policies are failing to boost the quality of public services, the beleaguered taxpayer will continue paying through the nose for the public sector recruitment spree, while getting little or nothing in return, other than administrators administrating each other.

Or worse, fishermen hauled before the courts for landing a half dozen sprats for the cat; or tombstone checkers who flatten graves for health and safety lunacy; or zealous box-tickers who close down local abattoirs and add suffering to livestock sent for slaughter.

The consequences of combining more bureaucracy and more bureaucrats has been devastating. Our society and our entrepreneurs are being shackled by a culture of inspection.

Even the Government which recruited all these people and created the jobs has realised that there is a problem. It has set out plans, following the *Gershon Review,* to reduce the number of civil servants by 84,150 over a four year period.

Unfortunately, early feedback from departments suggests that these changes are happening very slowly, and that even on the most optimistic of interpretations the excess numbers are only being cut by half.

One of the most striking features of *Guardian Society,* which advertises public sector jobs every Wednesday, is the way in which the staggering sums are divided. Few of the positions advertised are poorly-paid – but those which pay least are the ones which seem to be the most useful.

A country needs social workers. They are indispensable front-line staff in an acute area of public service. We are hard-pushed, however, to explain why Britain needs to fill posts like:

'Supporting People Manager'
'Female Advocacy Manager'
'Antisocial Behaviour Co-ordinator'

Yet all these latter positions pay a salary above £30,000 a year (the person fortunate enough to be chosen as Supporting People Manager can make up to £46,548), while many social workers earn below £15,000.

It's not even as if the high salaries reflect unusually burdensome working hours. Time and again, jobs are advertised with the words 'Hours: 35 per week' and '37 hours per week'. Seven hour days, five days a week are frequently all that is required to take home the handsome salaries up for grabs – normal working hours, or less.

Jobs that neglect to mention short hours in their advertisements often have other substantial perks – and many offer both.

'Up to 31 days annual leave'
'+ generous benefits'
'plus 10% car allowance'
'+ car'
'£1,296 loyalty bonus after one year's service'
'plus fringe allowance'

Jobs paying salaries of £40,000 and offering 'additional payment for travelling time and costs incurred' jump out of the pages of *Guardian Society* with monotonous and frightening regularity.

All manner of benefits denied to private sector employees are extended to those who get public sector jobs. In particular, generous pensions terms – a burden for the taxpayer that continues long after the substantial salary costs have been paid.

All those 'advocacy managers' and 'behaviour co-ordinators' add up to over three quarters of a billion pounds of taxpayers' money every year. This money would be better spent on more front-line staff or lower taxes. Taxpayers deserve better.

Top 10 Non-Jobs

The Daily Telegraph runs a fantastic 'Non-Job of the Week' column written by Jim Levi. Here are our Top 10 non-jobs from last year.

Director of Understanding and Enjoyment New Forest National Park Authority - circa £50,000 per annum plus benefits

Records Management & Information Compliance Adviser South West of England Regional Development Agency - £26,304 rising to £32,808

Regional Culture in Rural Development Manager East Midlands Development Agency - £29,000 to £32,000

Project Development Worker, E-portfolios South West Opportunities for Older People - £20,043 to £27,000

Community Compost Development Officer The Community Recycling Network for Scotland - £23,739 to £25,857 per annum

Policy Development Manager Banstead Borough Council - £37,164 to £46,410 (with possible progression to £52,500)

Street Scene Outreach Officer Enfield Council - from £24,114 to £25,602

Co-ordinator, Local Area Structures and Arrangements Framework Wolverhampton City Council - £34,566 to £39,303 (pay award pending)

International Affairs Coordinator Greater London Authority - £27,489 plus interest-free season ticket and bicycle loan

Relationship Manager The Office of Government Commerce - £55,000 a year plus benefits (more for an exceptional candidate)

How to Spot a Non-Job: The Giveaway Phrases

". . . develop the ongoing quality assurance of this exciting, relatively new programme."

". . . assist us in raising our priority neighbourhoods to at least average national levels in terms of service provision."

". . . work in pioneering areas to explore the path towards a new era of total learning."

". . . help us put the structures in place to ensure the involvement of local people."

". . . work with us to achieve a sustainable approach to local democracy."

". . . draw up action plans for new-look learning structures to meet the complex and rapidly evolving skills challenges of the next two decades."

". . . plan and coordinate the delivery of a national community compost strategy and provide ongoing support to community compost projects."

". . . have the time, space, money and support to push at the boundaries of knowledge and practice."

". . . develop a strategy to guide the future management of countryside and green spaces to ensure they underpin the wider renaissance vision of a city of learning, culture, tourism and high technology industries."

Public Sector Pensions

We are, of course, still paying for public sector non-job employees even when they stop not working for us.

The Gordon Brown raid on private pension funds now stands at £7.3 billion a year. That is the level of tax that the Chancellor hiked onto our retirement funds. Britain used to be at the top of the pensions league in Europe. Now, thanks to Brown's robbery, we have already slipped to sixth place. Many readers will remember pensions advisers telling you that you will need to put more money into the fund after 1997 merely to stay at the same level. Those who couldn't afford to will be poorer when they retire.

It is a scandal. Because at the same time, there are now an extra 700,000 public sector pensions to pay since 1997, and with bigger pay packets to boot, it means the taxpayer has to fork out for a bigger pensions bill.

88 per cent of public sector workers are members of a final salary pension scheme, but only 16 per cent of private sector employees are. The state, meaning you the taxpayer, pays.

So given that people are living longer, it will come as no surprise to hear that our pension liabilities have soared, threatening to saddle taxpayers with huge tax bills. Official estimates put the current value of tomorrow's pension promises at £460 billion (March 2004). The actuarial profession as at March 2005 puts it nearer to £690 billion.

No money having been set aside, taxes may have to rise by up to 5p in the pound to cover the shortfall. Council tax bills are already rising, partly to plug deficits in local authority schemes.

In an attempt to bring costs under control, ministers proposed in 2005 that the public sector pension based on final salary should be replaced with one based on average earnings during a career. At the same time, the retirement age would rise from 60 to 65. Later in the year, the Government caved in to the unions, and these changes aren't going to be fully implemented for nearly a decade. Public sector pension payments are still set to be index-linked, so they will rise in line with inflation. State workers will still not have to worry about investment performance.

Under the changes, anyone in a public sector job today will not be affected by the Government's reforms. A 21 year old civil servant can look forward to retiring in 2045 at the age of 60 without the new regulations having any effect on his generous pension terms. With life expectancy rising – a non-smoker can reach his mid 80s – that individual could easily spend a quarter of his life on his super-generous, publicly-funded, final salary pension. And, of course, there's the added bonus that local government staff outlive the retired private sector!

Government employees should not be treated better than their counterparts in the private sector. It is time to close the Government's final salary pension schemes.

The Deficit

According to a recent Parliamentary Question, local government pension schemes in England and Wales have assets of £80 billion and liabilities of £107 billion. This translates to a shortfall of £27 billion. No prizes for guessing who will foot the bill.

Overall, existing public sector pensions have run up an estimated £690 billion bill for 3 million current workers. That's an extra £300 for every household for the next 30 years, or £11,000 for every man, woman and child.

The public sector therefore accounts for around 18 per cent of jobs but 36 per cent of pensions. Raising the retirement age to 65 and ending generous final salary schemes could save £7 billion. These schemes used to be generous because public sector employees were generally lower paid than those in the private sector. As we have seen, that justification is no longer valid.

But even these figures may need to be revised. A study by the Institute of Economic Affairs has found that the government has public sector pension liabilities of £817 billion, well above previous estimates. The IEA study, by Neil Record, an investment manager and former Bank of England economist, tried to assess the pension liability that the government would have to put on its books if it were a company. Its final figure is equivalent to 69 per cent of GDP (the turnover of the economy in a given year).

If you listen very, very carefully, you can hear the sound of someone trying to find a paddle, echoing around a creek.

The Royal Family

Royalty costs. The only country in which it doesn't is where the monarch cycles to work in the morning and holidays on a canal in a rented peddalo. And who wants that? That said, there are occasions when you wonder if taxpayers' money is being properly spent on this venerable institution.

As ever, when the criticism is flying, it pays to dig beneath the surface. The £300,000 it cost to charter a Boeing 757 to fly Prince Charles' entourage to the United States, for instance, might have been offset by £50,000 recouped from the accompanying journalists, and thus been more cost-effective than taking over the whole upper deck of a scheduled plane.

The bill for the Queen's three garden parties comes to £500,000 a year. But then, as *The Times* pointed out, that covers 20,000 sandwiches, 9,000 scones, and 27,000 cups of tea, which is an awful lot of refreshment for an awful lot of guests.

Less defensible are the stories about Prince Andrew chartering flights to play golf. The cost of hiring aeroplanes and helicopters over a twelve month period reportedly ran to £325,000. Then again, at least he flew one as a decoy for Exocet missiles in a real war, unlike the Labour ministers who like to jaunt around the globe at public expense. Margaret Beckett spent £120,000 on overseas travel in 2004, which was more than Jack Straw – and he runs the Foreign Office. Certain ministers use the Queen's Flight like a personal taxi service, e.g. when the PM flew off to sun himself in Egypt.

Let's put this in perspective. The gross cost of the Royal Family was £41 million in 2003, or 60p for each person in the UK.

- £9 million was the Civil List – money paid to the Queen and Prince Philip in return for surrendering the Crown Estates.

- £27 million was 'grants-in-aid'. Basically this is the cost of maintaining royal buildings, which would be maintained whether we had a monarchy or not.

- £5 million was the Queen's Flight and Royal Train, also used by ministers.

The Queen also gets income from the Privy Purse, which is income from her remaining land, the Duchy of Lancaster. This costs the taxpayer nothing, but she pays tax on it.

Contrast this £43 million cost with the royal revenue paid into the Treasury which is estimated at £168 million:

- £163 million from Crown Estates' 300,000 acres of land. A majority of income comes from land in Central London.

- £2 million in tax from the Duchy of Lancaster.

- £3 million in tax from Prince Charles's Duchy of Cornwall.

This is money that the Treasury gets *from* the monarchy.

Even if we ignore the tourism and business gains, we find the net gain to the country from having a monarchy comes to £127 million a year – or approximately £2.18 per person per year. The monarchy not only pays for itself, but also buys everyone in the country a drink as well.

The European Union

Strangely, there is a degree of uncertainty about how much money the UK pays annually for the privilege of belonging to the European Union.

Whenever the Treasury has started to do the sums, the guillotine has come down from Ken Clarke or Gordon Brown. It is clearly somewhat controversial.

We will steer clear of the cost/benefit argument of belonging to the EU. That analysis has been done many times over the last couple of years, and the conclusions are ugly. It is worth a book in its own right – and some excellent ones have been written.*

Ultimately, it remains a political decision as to whether you think forking out the money, choking your businesses with red tape, and trashing your common law traditions, is worth whatever imaginary benefits you think might be found lurking at the bottom of the EU pork barrel.

In this book, we will just concern ourselves with the historic and current cost to British taxpayers of EU membership, and look at the institutionalised waste and extravagance that ramps it up.

Britain's contributions to EU finances

On the plus side, we do at least have the Fontainebleau Rebate that was won with Maggie Thatcher's handbag. This brings back

---

* See 'Further Reading', p225.

a sizeable chunk of the money paid into the EU by Britain – typically between three to five billion pounds a year – but the maths is such that part of the rebate is deducted from other money that we could also claim in grants from the budget. Since the Treasury people would end up paying for a large chunk of many of the grants we could claim, they don't like other departments applying for our money back. This bit is not so good.

Even after the Rebate – diminished to the tune of £1 billion per year by Tony Blair's budget deal last December – the UK remains the second largest net contributor after the Germans, who are, after all, twenty million more numerous than us, and who all drive Audis.

We as UK taxpayers have been net contributors to the EU every year since we joined. The one year we weren't so much was 1975 which, coincidentally, was the year we had a referendum on whether or not we wanted to stay in. It is estimated that, purely in terms of direct contributions to the Brussels budget, by 2007-08 we will have paid a gross £216 billion, and a net £92 billion. So we have handed over, for keeps, the equivalent of eighteen months of the entire NHS mega budget. To what purpose has this money been put? Why, to subsidise other countries, of course.

Couple this with the fact that the EU budget is now running at £70 billion or so a year, it is only right that the British taxpayer should feel that their money – because it is *their* money – should be being spent wisely, prudently, efficiently and in their interest.

If only. Let's start with fraud and mismanagement.

EU Fraud and Mismanagement

According to a report from the EU's own Internal Audit Service (IAS), an estimated £4.5 billion of the EU's annual budget is wasted each year. Before EU enlargement, the UK contributed €10.1 billion of the total €77.7 billion contributions from the Member States, or 13.1 per cent. Thirteen per cent of the £4.5 billion annual waste is £589.5 million of EU fraud and mismanagement paid for by British taxpayers. And that's using the EU's own figures – there are far worse estimates out there.

The political will to do something about EU fraud is lamentable. For eleven years now, the EU Court of Auditors has declined to sign off almost all of the accounts. Whistleblowers have been emerging from just about every EU institution, reporting on endemic system abuse, mismanagement, rule fiddling, and – when they complain – have been trampled on by senior management who are determined to resort to every method in the book, including intimidation, to suppress the truth.

It would make a great novel if the EU itself weren't so boring.

There have been, for instance, a series of allegations about millions siphoned off from the Palestinian Authority to keep key figures in furs. €1 billion from the clean up of nuclear power plants in Russia is still reported lost. Aid sent to help the victims of oppression in Zimbabwe is being sent for an exchange rate via the Harare Central Bank, so it is supporting the regime. As a whistleblower has revealed to us, it goes all the way down the system, to petty larceny by minor staff in Brussels, and people claiming up to £12,000 a year in false expenses with bosses turning a blind eye.

At least the Court of Auditors is picking up on some of this. Take some of the conclusions it reached in its last-but-one Annual Report:

- 38 per cent of Portuguese suckler cows for which money was claimed didn't exist.

- 90,000 tonnes of imaginary olives were produced in Italy. These pseudo-olives would fill enough articulated trucks to form a nose to tail traffic jam 36 miles long.

- Massive amounts of detected fraud is being written off. Of the €3.1 billion reported since 1971, only 17 per cent has been retrieved. There is "no disincentive to frivolous appeals" by those caught red-handed so they have no qualms about making such appeals, and get away with it.

- The Commission is too scared to blacklist culprits because it is afraid of being sued.

- Europeans don't like the taste or smell of subsidised EU tobacco (which is why it gets dumped onto the Third World).

- German members of the Economic and Social Committee were fiddling their expenses.

- Senior Third World officials were making money from EU export stability funds.

The latest Annual Report, covering 2004, is equally damning:

- Officials supposed to be carrying out CAP inspections were faking visits for the records, so that €1 billion of grants was in serious question.

- One farmer falsely claimed for a herd of sheep that had supposedly been hit by disease and eaten by wolves.

- Money is being wasted on badly-managed forestry schemes that may die anyway because of lack of nurturing grants to municipalities.

- Some member states have implemented risk systems that, strangely, find less fraud in the CAP than completely random checks.

- 96 per cent of Spanish "own resources" debt to the EU is being written off. This compares with 10 per cent of UK debt believed to be irretrievable.

- The Commission is only auditing one fifth of the number of contractors set out in its own targets.

- Reports of systematic errors found in Commission audits are being lost in the system.

- Timekeeping was being replaced by guesstimates in a number of contracts.

- The EU is still paying for fishing in Greenland waters for non-existent fish.

- Errors on a new computer have led to staff being overpaid and the system being vulnerable to fraud. €1.9 million has been reclaimed.

- Staff have been paid accommodation subsidies despite providing no proof they are entitled to the allowance.

- Two retired Eurocrats were caught claiming the UK residents' allowance despite having moved to another country.

- A and B grade staff have a total of 11,800 days outstanding of overtime, for which retiring personnel will be paid. In one month alone that cost €95,000.

So much for fraud and mismanagement by EU employees and contractors. Let's turn to the costs of the institutions themselves.

EU Institutions

The EU machine is currently constructing new buildings to cope with enlargement. Historically, art has gotten the better of cost effectiveness. The Belgian architect who has designed the new Council of Ministers building has come up with a "dancing pregnant goddess" that looks like a glass nuclear reactor inside an outer shell. Its estimated cost is presently £135 million.

Then there is the EU library system. This is a very exclusive beast because it is not open to the general public. Nor is it very popular with staff or MEPs, especially the one which is based in Luxembourg, which is in a different country from the majority of personnel. The Luxembourg library saw 459 book loans last year, which works out as costing the taxpayer £2,138 per book. The Brussels library is positively cost-effective in comparison at a mere £1,379 per book loaned. But that's still more expensive than a full set of the *Encyclopedia Britannica.*

The European Parliament doesn't run itself, of course. There are 180 ushers at three EP sites. They are also available to help out at political group meetings. This makes them expensive bouncers. Some of them are delightfully jobsworthy, such as the one who turned away a Privy Counsellor during the drafting of the EU Constitution because he didn't have his security pass on him, until an accompanying member of staff lent him his own.

As a point of interest, the House of Commons makes do with 33 doorkeepers.

The European Commission doesn't have ushers. It has security. With machine guns, sniper rifles and silencers, but that's a different scandal. We're more interested in how much it spends on running its own saunas (one is reserved for VIPs) to keep the Scandinavians from getting homesick. Naturally, being the European Commission, there is a ten point code of conduct for staff to use it.

It's not known how big these saunas are. They must be fairly crowded, because as of 1st September 2005, there were 26,163 people working in the European Commission. La crème de la crème. It doesn't sound a lot to run an entire continent, but they are merely the ketchup on the cheeseburger of Europe's national civil servants. And they're on pop star wages. Remember that numbers belie power.

With so many scandals going on, you need to keep leaks out of the newspapers. The EU has a generous number of press officers for its size. There are 13 employed by the Council of Ministers (not counting those actually employed by each Minister); 27 in the Commission; 53 in the European Parliament; the European Court of Justice's 8; 3 in the advisory institutions; and a paltry 1 for the Court of Auditors and 1 for the European ombudsman – the bodies that actually do some good. Maybe that explains it.

The **advisory committees** do need their press people. The Economic and Social Committee and the Committee of the Regions are widely ridiculed as expensive talking shops for corporate business and trade unionists on the one hand, and local councillors on junkets on the other. They write reports that are ignored unless they happen to provide spurious justification for some daft law that is going through. Advisory committees cost £115 million a year. No one would notice if they were shut down.

Convincing people is big business in Brussels. Take the EU persuasion machine. Detailed research from the Bruges Group has revealed that over €100 million is being spent annually to convince people to love the EU. Even now, there is €6 million set aside in the 2006 draft budget for promoting the EU Constitution, something which two referendums have rejected.

On top of that, there is the £600 million that the EU hands out to lobby groups every year. These have been criticised by Green MEPs as being in the main "radical left-wing NGOs that are opposed to free markets and competition", and the grants are running wild and free. In other words, there is a real industry in the EU funding organisations that are campaigning against its own policies.

Whatever your political views, this is not joined-up government; rather, it is a parody of democracy, and a total waste of resources.

EU Bureaucrats

Fighting against the tide of public opinion is a demanding job, one that demands that EU bureaucrats receive generous compensatory perks. One such perk is the European Schools Network for EU civil servants. There are thirteen of these schools, catering for 20,000 pupils. They carry a £160 million annual price tag. The UK share of this bill is disproportionately high, because we pay for all the UK nationals who are teachers, and English language speakers are preferred.

The civil servants who benefit are already being paid on a 16 per cent tax rate, with big allowances and salaries. The average take home pay for A grade Commission staff is £70,000 a year. Many would be able to afford private schooling for their children if they didn't want them to go to local schools.

Nor is it right that these schools have as their mission statement support for EU integration, effectively indoctrinating these children at public expense. In other circumstances it would be like the system forming a future Soviet cadre.

In addition to the generous salaries, tax rates, and kids' schooling, EU bureaucrats enjoy seven additional allowances, plus a pension scheme after ten years. They tend to get Friday afternoons off plus numerous Belgian bank holidays. They also benefit from an exceedingly benign 'correction coefficient' if they live in a country which is more expensive than Belgium – in Britain that means a 42 per cent wage hike. It also means a £303 million pensions bill for the taxpayer with the average A Grade staff getting a pension approaching £40,000 p.a.

All in all, it's a thoroughly agreeable lifestyle for the EU bureaucrats, but less so for the taxpayers who have to fund it. And yet, believe it or not, these bureaucrats are mere babes in the wood when it comes to exploiting the system. The masters of the art, the real plunderers of the EU coffers, are the MEPs.

MEPs

Each MEP is estimated to cost taxpayers £2.4 million a year, in comparison to just over £375,000 for each MP. Some of the difference reflects the cost of translation and international travel in an MEP's work, but a great deal of it pays for their chauffeur service and other unnecessary expenditure. If the spending for each of the 78 British MEPs alone was arbitrarily cut to £1 million, this would save taxpayers just over £109 million a year.

One obvious money-saving step would be to scrap the MEPs' buildings in Luxembourg and Strasbourg and concentrate activity in Brussels. Nearly four thousand trunks move backwards and forwards between the offices every month. Having two sets of offices means having, for instance, two sets of linked computers. Staff travel and accommodation alone racks up £6 million in costs. Scrapping the additional EP buildings would save EU taxpayers £120 million a year.

MEP allowances are an invitation to fiddle. One UKIP MEP got caught last year claiming £36,000 for a researcher who was actually paid only one sixth of that amount. There is a lot of money slushing around.

At the last check, there was:

- €3,785 per month (half if you slack in attending plenary sittings) to cover office expenses and domestic travel.

- A travel and expenses allowance to cover the cost of getting to MEP sessions.

- Up to €3,736 annual travel allowance to cover scooting off anywhere in the world in performance of duties. This means political jollies, or if you are Glenys Kinnock, travelling to a Third World Sunshine Capital only to time it so that you find yourself in the middle of a revolution. Motorcades may be put on for you by the resident dictator as an optional extra.

- Subsistence Allowance at €268 per day for each day of attendance at official meetings (or half of this plus accommodation/breakfast expenses for meetings held outside the EU).

- Secretarial Assistance Allowance of up to €12,576 per month to cover the expenses arising from the engagement or employment of one or more assistants. These are often relatives of the MEP.

- Up to €50 per week taxi allowance.

- A generous pension *plus* a two-for-one publicly funded

matching on a second pension. Bad investment practices mean there is currently a £29 million pensions fund hole. Added to which, the Court of Auditors has discovered that the second fund is illegal, and as it has no rules, it is an unfunded black hole liability.

Your secret glimpse behind the scenes

During the course of writing *The Bumper Book*, the TaxPayers' Alliance was able to get hold of a hidden tome for the first time. Previously, the chances of finding it were only slightly greater than seeing Glenn Miller riding Shergar down the streets of Atlantis. It's the same old story. You can get hold of it, if you know it exists, if you know what it's called, if you happen to be one of a dozen people on the European Parliament Conference of Presidents who can access it.

Astonishingly, without even resorting to bribery, we can now reveal some of the truly hidden perks of life in Brussels. The following are examples of benefits and schemes available to MEPs. Many of them were perks that *all* EU bureaucrats were already getting when some bright new MEP found out about them. So you can add the cost of applying these perks to thousands of Brussels staffers as well.

Cars and Chauffeurs

The European Parliament (EP) has a stock of official cars and a supply of chauffeurs. Some are reserved for bigwigs, while others form a pool for MEPs to get in, around and out of Brussels and Strasbourg.

The following office-holders get one automatically:

- The President of the EP
- The Secretary-General (Chief bureaucrat)
- The Chairmen of each political group

Everyone else waits in a queue or books. According to the regulations (though sensibly not in practice), staff cannot accompany a member in an otherwise empty car.

It is customary to tip.

The costs of the car itself are set, the President's at a maximum €51,000, the other head honchos' at €46,000. Enough for a spanking new XJ Jaguar. The tariff can include GPS but top of the range carphone add-ons can go in as extras.

On retirement

As you can imagine, having got used to these perks of office, European bureaucrats are reluctant to give them up. The regulations are touchingly sympathetic on this score – well, they are to ex-Presidents. On retirement, former Presidents of the European Parliament continue to have:

- 3 months use of a chauffeur-driven limousine; followed by
- 9 months of priority chauffeur from the MEP pool.

And, of course they still need somewhere to sit, so they get:

- The continued use of a large office, equal in size to that of Committee chairmen; and

- Two and a half years of extra secretarial allowance, so they can write letters to *Der Spiegel* in green ink.

Furniture

Extremely strict rules govern the amount and type of furniture issued to each MEP. Regulation 2.2.2 allows them one office table, one movable chest of drawers, one swivel chair, two visitor's chairs, one desk lamp, and one office storage system comprising "one set of shelves, 3 tray shelves and integrated wastepaper bin, personal storage unit, bookcase, TV stand and reclining armchair". Similar rules apply to their support staff. The length of the document is the same as the American Declaration of Independence. Perhaps the administrators felt guilty after all the publicity surrounding the £7,000 shower units installed in every office.

Courses

MEPs can attend courses on languages and on how to use their computer. The five main languages are taught by a teacher who comes to the MEP's office. Teaching costs are fully reimbursed.

If an MEP wants to learn a more exotic language – say, Maltese – he can enrol in an outside language school and recoup not only the tuition fees, but also travel and subsistence costs. Valetta's very nice at this time of year.

The budget limit on language courses is €5,000 a year for each MEP and €1,500 on computer training. He gets up to two return trips paid for to Sunsville, and up to twenty days on half-allowance.

Budget Line 3701

It sounds like the latest bootstrapped no-frills airline, but Budget Line 3701 is, in fact, a pleasing regulation under which MEPs can claim subsidies for a wide range of promotional initiatives. Pleasing for the MEPs, that is.

Much of this cherished wad (about €41 million a year, equivalent to €55,738 per MEP) goes towards supporting political activities by the political parties in Brussels. Published material, also known as propaganda, must carry the European Parliament's logo on it.

Expenditure is also authorised for hiring offices and staff, staff entertainment, MEPs' entertainment, stationery and stamps, setting up a database, conferences in nice places, "guests" (which sounds dubious), advertising and legal bills.

Some examples of spending in the past include T-shirts and umbrellas with the political group's logo on, and spending large amounts getting involved in other people's referendum campaigns (which is expressly authorised by the rules).

Insurance

MEPs get the following kinds of insurance paid for them:

- Accident (including when they are not on public duty)
- Life
- Theft and loss during public duties. Worldwide coverage with an excess of only about twenty pounds.

This equates to a limit of:

- €250,000 if they die
- €375,000 if they are permanently crippled
- €7,500 of medical cover

Agreeably, the life insurance matures if an MEP has served two terms. An MEP hitting 60 or retiring from politics then gets up to €15,338.

Medical Expenses

These types of treatment are subsidised:

- Acupuncture
- Kinesitherapy
- 28 days of convalescence a year
- 21 days a year of "thermal cure" i.e. going to a spa

An MEP or a family member gets 80 per cent of expenses repaid if the treatment can be gained from the NHS but he or she prefers to go private.

Sick Children

Spouses and dependent children of MEPs, and seemingly the civil servants, get medical cover under the Joint Sickness Insurance Scheme. The ceiling is €30,000 per family member.

The policy covers all the usual medical ailments, but also things like spectacles and teeth correctors.

Qualifying family members include anyone aged under 26 who is still a student. The wording allows for coverage to extend to illegitimate love children not resident with the father. Handy for the politicians, then.

Spectacles

For MEPs, bureaucrats, their spouses and dependents:

- Up to €544 for the lenses and €63.46 for the frame
- Contact lenses are subsidised by up to €148.75 per lens
- Disposable contact lenses €300.00 every 24 months

Health Props

- Hearing aid allowance: €923.41 plus free batteries
- Orthopaedic footware and soles (two pairs biannually): €359.96 per pair
- Maternity belts, knee bandages, ankle supports, lumbar girdles: *at cost*
- Artificial limbs and segments thereof, crutches and walking sticks: *at cost*
- Wheelchairs: *at cost*
- Post-operative nursing allowance: up to €85.75 a day with option on home nursing
- Convalescence allowance: €29.16 a day for a max of 28 days
- Thermal baths attendance allowance: €20.21 a day for up to 21 days

Electrotherapy

MEPs and relatives are each allowed up to 60 sessions a year of a combination of the following: *diadynamic currents, radar, ionisation, short-wave treatment and other special currents.*

Kinesitherapy

MEPs and relatives are each allowed up to 60 sessions a year of: *medical massage, medical gymnastics, ante- and post-natal gymnastics, mobilisation, rehabilitation, mechanotherapy, traction, mud baths, hydromassage and hydrotherapy.*

Aerosol Therapy

MEPs and relatives are each allowed up to 30 sessions a year of: *inhalation, insufflation, irrigation and nebulisation/nasal spray.*

Beam Therapy

MEPs and relatives are each allowed up to 30 sessions a year of: *infra-red rays and ultrasonics.*

Acupuncture

MEPs and relatives are each allowed up to 30 sessions a year of acupuncture carried out by a doctor.

Teeth

Whack a Brussels bureaucrat round the chops with a two-by-four, and the expensive cosmetic dentistry that follows will be paid from your pocket, not his. Opposite is the dental allowance in all its awesome fullness.

Disability Pension

If the Invalidity Committee recognises you as taking early MEP retirement because of disability, you can get a temporary or permanent pension of about £40,000 per year. This is reduced by other pension schemes if you have been an MEP for a long time.

Maximum reimbursement per tooth (in Euros)

Fixed prostheses

Gold crown, plastic jacket	185.92
Plastic bridge tooth element	185.92
Gold inlay, moulded false stump	185.92
Pivot crown	185.92
Richmond crown or ceramic and metal crown, veneer or ceramic and metal bridge tooth element	185.92
Gold and porcelain bridge tooth element	185.92
Spring attachment	185.92
Hinge	96.67

Removable prostheses

Full set of dentures, upper or lower (14 teeth, plastic plate)	674.14
Partial dentures with synthetic resin plastic plate:	
- base plate	149.72
- per tooth	46.72
- per clasp	33.58
Metal prosthesis (chrome cobalt):	
- plate and clasp	311.98
- per tooth	104.37

Repairs

Repairs to the plastic plate	60.00
Addition of a tooth or clasp to the plastic plate	67.31
Rebasing (upper or lower)	267.97
(40% of full set of dentures)	
Remounting (upper or lower)	505.70
(75% of full set of dentures)	

Subject to the conditions laid down in the above scale, the cost of temporary prostheses shall be reimbursed up to a maximum of 23.38. Periodontosis charges shall be reimbursed up to a maximum of 297.47 per sextant.

Still awake? Welcome to the psyche of Brussels!

Survivor's Pension

The wives of deceased MEPs continue to receive about £36,000 a year. This is weighted to their country of residence.

Children

Pregnant MEPs get three months off before and six months off after birth, on standard pay. It is likely that male MEPs will soon benefit from generous paternity leave as well.

Visitors to the Inmates

MEPs get the opportunity to indoctrinate up to 90 constituents a year on how wonderful their job is. This is very useful as part of a package to get themselves re-elected. The visitors come to Brussels, or even better Strasbourg, or, if the member hates them, Luxembourg. In any event, they get the sales pitch from the MEP and then from a Visitor's Centre wonk, and then are forced to visit the European Parliament's public gallery for a bit, which hopefully will teach them there's no such thing as a free lunch. The Directorate-General of Information itself can invite "opinion formers" in order to indoctrinate them at public expense. Travel and meals are subsidised.

Euroscola Programme

Schoolchildren are brought to the European Parliament to hold mock debates and votes. Sounds a bit like the normal European Parliament. Classes are arbitrarily divided into five squabbling groups. This also sounds just like the real thing. Perhaps the children would do a better and cheaper job?

The Supreme Waste Award

We now take the opportunity to make an award for what we consider to be the pinnacle of waste. In making the award we commend the European Union for coming up with the most pointless perk ever encountered in TaxPayers' Alliance research. As far as we can tell, it has never been made public before. Turn the page to find out who the winner is . . .

The TaxPayers' Alliance

Supreme Waste Award

is hereby awarded to:

MEPs and Brussels bureaucrats

for

A glass eye allowance

Citation: Although counting themselves amongst the highest paid civil servants on the continent of Europe, and the politicians in receipt of amongst the most generous system of perks, allowances and pay, the elite of Brussels have managed to wangle for themselves a genuinely sublime example of taxpayers needlessly picking up the bill.

For reasons of no known historic origin nor rationale, said elite have decided that "the cost of artificial eyes shall be reimbursed" for MEPs and EU civil servants and their immediate family.

Signed: A. Taxpayer

Section Four

Waste and Extravagance in Perspective

The European Central Bank found that if the UK's public spending were as efficient as that of the US, or Japan, the Government could spend 16 per cent less than it currently does, while still producing the same level of public services.

The table below shows the comparative performance of different countries, with the UK ranking well down the league. Our score of 0.84 compared to the US, Japan and Luxembourg's 1.00 gives rise to the 16 per cent deficit.

Country	Efficiency	Country	Efficiency
United States	1.00	Denmark	0.62
Japan	1.00	Sweden	0.57
Luxembourg	1.00	Canada	0.75
Switzerland	0.95	Finland	0.61
Norway	0.73	New Zealand	0.83
Ireland	0.96	United Kingdom	0.84
Australia	0.99	Germany	0.72
Austria	0.67	Belgium	0.66
Netherlands	0.72	Spain	0.80
Iceland	0.87	France	0.64

Chris Rock Talks Taxes

The stand-up comedian and Hollywood actor speaks out on tax:

"One thing Clinton did was raise taxes. The messed up thing about taxes is, we don't "pay" taxes. The government TAKES them. You get your check and money is GONE! It was not no option! That ain't a payment that's a JACK!

Every week they take money out of your check, then they want some MORE money in April. What kind of gangster **** is that?! Why didn't they just take the money they needed in the first place? Instead of coming to me like a damn crack head saying, 'Remember that money I borrowed before? I need a little bit more." UNCLE SAM IS ON THE PIPE! The worst part about it is that we pay taxes for **** we don't even use:

Fire Department: My house ain't burning! I keep the sprinklers on 24 hours a day. Gotta nice MOIST house!

Police Department: I never called a cop in my life! If something go down I have a GUN. I'll handle it my damn self. And if I do ever need the police, I'll be happy to write them a check: "Somebody broke into my house. Here you go."

School tax: I don't have any kids!! Why am I paying school tax?! I know some of y'all got kids...But do you think I give a damn how dumb YOUR kids are? I don't care if your kid is in 10th grade with coloring books. I wear condoms for a reason...trying to save a few dollars. When I get some kids then I'll care and then I'll pay! But now, I have to pay for everyone else's kids to go to school.

Social Security tax: Why are black people paying Social Security? I won't get the money till I'm 65... Meanwhile, the average black man dies at 54. Hypertension, high blood pressure, LAPD, crazy white boys...something will get your ass! Black people should be able to get Social Security at 30.

How they goin to force you to save your own damn money? They should ask us if we want them to take Social Security. A white man should come to your job and say 'would you like us to save money for you when u get old?' NO, I want the **** NOW!

I use to work at McDonalds making minimum wage. When you make minimum wage, that means the job doesn't give a damn about you. They don't care about your Christmas, they don't care if your kid got shoes on. Boss talkin bout 'Hey, how you doing?' You know how the **** I'm doing! I'm doing BAD, that's how I'm doing. How can I be doing anything with this lil bit of money u paying me? When you make minimum wage that's like the job saying 'Hey, if we could pay you less, we would...But it's against the law!'

I would get $200 a week and they would take out $50 in taxes. That's a lot of money if you only making $200. That's like kicking Wednesday and Thursday in the ass. What do you get with that $50? All the free street light in world. As far as I'm concerned, give everybody a candle! Just give me back my $50. I hate checks too. I hate the fact that they put two different amounts of money on your check. Its like: ...

This is the amount of money you bust your ass for: And this how much you gonna get:

Why are they showing me this money I'm not going to get? I don't want to see that! Don't take off your clothes and not have sex with me.

If you work at McDonalds making fries, they still tax you. I think it's obvious that if you make french fries for a living that you deserve a break - TODAY! It's not fair. If you're the mop-up boy at a peep show, it's obvious the government is not working for you.

Let's get rid of taxes. Taxes are why we left England. White people said, 'They're taxing everything. Let's go.' That was over 300 years ago. They thought they were doing a good thing. Now taxes are even higher. And there's no place left to go!"

© Chris Rock

Understanding Taxation

"The hardest thing in the world to understand is taxation."

Albert Einstein

Below is an example of a Laffer curve. Hand up who knows what a Laffer curve is?

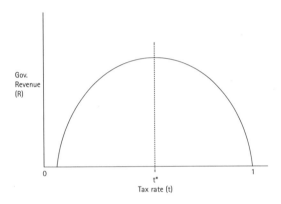

Is it:

(a) A cross section of Yorkshire

(b) The top bit of a hard boiled egg

(c) An economic model showing t* as the best rate of taxation

All those who answered (c), get five points. Top economist Arthur Laffer drew this sketch on a napkin over dinner to prove a point. The theory runs like this:

If the government taxes you for every penny, then it quickly ends up with no revenue, because there's no point in you getting out of bed in the morning. You do no work, and it gets no taxes.

At the same time, as the tax rate rises, the incentive to fiddle or bypass the system becomes greater.

It is no coincidence that cigarette smuggling is a major activity in the highly taxed Western world, from North America through to Western Europe. Look at the comparative prices of a packet of 20 Marlboro on the street:

€6.95	€4.70	€1.88	€1.66	92c	50c
Britain	Germany	Czech Rep.	Poland	Belarus	Russia

The mark-up actually results in lost revenue, because there is a financial reward for the smuggler and the buyer by avoiding excise. That's why in 2000, an estimated one packet in five smoked in the UK had dodged taxes, which meant £2.5 billion in lost revenue. Sure, there may be health benefits in making it cheaper to smoke truffles than tobacco, but let's not kid ourselves that the Treasury has our wellbeing uppermost in its mind when it slaps an extra couple of pence on every year. The double irony is that most smuggled cigarettes were actually made in the UK in the first place.

Now, back to the Laffer curve, which drops the further you go to the left in the lower taxes direction. Obviously, if government doesn't tax you at all, then it doesn't get any money because it's not getting any taxes.

So the point at which government *maximises* revenue lies somewhere in between, where the incentive to make money and pay taxes outweighs the disincentive.

Looking at the curve, if you are being taxed today at a given rate, it doesn't necessarily follow that putting up the taxes will increase the amount of money that government will get. But if taxes are lowered, it might mean (depending on where you are on the curve) that people want to work harder and make more money. So although the government's share of the revenue drops with lower taxes, the total take increases, and everybody wins.

What this in turn means is that people who continually bang the drum for higher taxes ought to stop and think.

Lower taxation encourages more work and investment, which may well bring in more tax revenue, and it also increases private wealth. It makes society richer, better able to look after itself, reduces dependency on the state, and increases the amount of money which government can use for good causes.

At the TaxPayers' Alliance, we believe that we are on the right-hand side of the curve and sliding down the wrong way. Cutting taxes would therefore actually boost public spending and increase funding opportunities for health and education.

So the next time someone tells you you're being selfish if you want lower taxes, tell them to go climb the Laffer curve!

"My money goes to my agent, then to my accountant, and from him to the tax man."

Glenda Jackson

The Postcode Lottery

Tax spending isn't fair.

Depending on where you live in the country, the Government is spending a highly variable amount of its tax receipts on you. These are the latest figures:

Region	Tax spend
Northern Ireland	£7,945
Scotland	£7,346
London	£7,166
Wales	£6,901
North East	£6,797
North West	£6,491
Yorkshire and Humberside	£5,980
West Midlands	£5,833
South West	£5,540
East Midlands	£5,498
South East	£5,164
Eastern	£5,151

Now, there's a strange correlation here. More money is being spent on the traditional Labour voting areas. A cynic would conclude that there is a clear link between places of higher welfare dependence and places which vote socialist. The one encourages the other.

It is certainly clear that England as a whole comes off worse than Scotland, Wales or Northern Ireland. Nationalists take note!

There is a further discrepancy. Money goes further in these better funded areas than it does in the expensive South of the country, so the value of the subsidy is even more unbalanced.

As a result, the South of England has, in itself, a lower share of Government spending than any rich country except South Korea. It is certainly lower than the US. The spending differential within the United Kingdom is as bad as that between West and East Germany after 1991.

This has resulted in the growth of what critics call a 'Soviet North', where there is a heavy dependence on state money. This is bad, because it is private enterprise that creates tax revenue in the first place, and which in turn is driven out by a large state sector. A larger state sector is also extremely difficult to reform unless a politician has real guts, because of the entrenched vested interests.

The figures in the table opposite show what proportion of each regional economy depends on tax money being spent.

Region	State spending
Northern Ireland	67%
Hungary on leaving Communism	60%
North East	59%
Wales	59%
Scotland	52%
North West	49%
Yorkshire	45%
West Midlands	45%
East Midlands	42%
South West	40%
Eastern	37%
London	34%
South East	33%

Scotland is clearly being heavily subsidised by England. The extent is so marked that if it ever became independent, and even if Edinburgh took over all the North Sea oil stocks, Scotland would still run a massive deficit.

English taxpayers subsidise free long term care for elderly Scots and the free Scottish university education. It would be fairer to scrap the English subsidy and force Scottish taxpayers to pay for the benefits that they receive. But then, that might create a backlash against socialism, which would change the political map of the North.

There may well be valid reasons for these subsidies. The poorer areas that are still coping with the aftermath of the decline of coal, steel and shipbuilding industries may still, twenty years on, have a case for increased state support. But politicians should be far more open about the fact that this is happening. At the moment, nobody appreciates the level of the subsidy, and this is bad for transparency.

The Flow of History

So much for the whos and wheres. What about the hows? *How* did we get here?

Some excellent work has been done over the last few years by Gabriel Stein of Lombard Street Research for the Adam Smith Institute, tracking how much money has been taken off us by the Government. The mechanism they use is *Tax Freedom Day.*

Imagine all the taxes you paid in a year were lumped together, and, starting from New Year's Day, you worked them off. Tax Freedom Day is the day in the year when you stop working for the Government and start working for yourself.

It's possible to calculate Tax Freedom Day over the years and thus to track how heavily the state has been taxing us over time. Over the page is a table showing how Tax Freedom Day has moved over the last 43 years, and a bar chart plotting the same dates.

Movement of Tax Freedom Day

The later the date in the year, the greater share of your money you are paying as taxes in that year.

1963	24-April	1977	28-May	1991	02-June
1964	24-April	1978	23-May	1992	29-May
1965	27-April	1979	25-May	1993	21-May
1966	02-May	1980	06-June	1994	22-May
1967	11-May	1981	14-June	1995	26-May
1968	18-May	1982	15-June	1996	25-May
1969	22-May	1983	12-June	1997	25-May
1970	26-May	1984	12-June	1998	28-May
1971	20-May	1985	11-June	1999	03-June
1972	14-May	1986	07-June	2000	04-June
1973	12-May	1987	04-June	2001	04-June
1974	28-May	1988	05-June	2002	26-May
1975	02-June	1989	02-June	2003	25-May
1976	31-May	1990	01-June	2004	27-May

Current *Tax Freedom Day* | 2005 | 31-May |

If you look at the bar chart on the opposite page, several points jump out:

- The tax burden rose fairly consistently from the mid 60s to the late 70s, a time of industrial strife and economic turbulence.

- After falling back in 1978 and 1979, the tax take started to rise again in the 80s, reaching a high in the recession of 1982 at a time when there were also sterling problems.

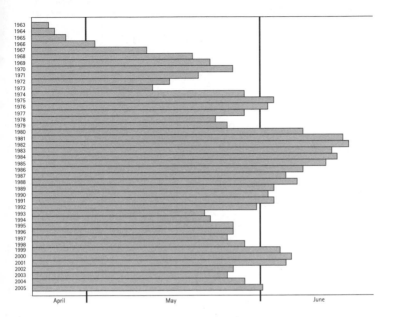

- From the mid 80s to the mid 90s tax fell, hitting a 35year low in 1993, when Tax Freedom Day was on 21st May.

- From the mid 90s to the present, the tax take has been on a rising trend, attributable solely to tax increases. There has been no hidden economic reason for this.

In plain English, Tax Freedom Day is slipping over time. As a result, we are worse off compared to our economic competitors. Behold the chart overleaf, which shows the international comparison.

Tax Freedom Day

International and Historical Comparison

TFD (2005)	Country
April 11	United States
May 5	Japan
May 15	Australia
May 26	**UK 1995**
May 27	Canada
May 31	**UK 2005**
June 6	Germany
June 7	**UK 2008**
July 5	France

You can see how, over time, we in Britain have seen our Tax Freedom Day drop in the calendar compared with other leading economies. The 2008 figure is based on the latest Budget projections.

So why has this changed over the past ten years?

The answer is pretty straightforward – increased taxes.

Increased Taxes

In 1995, income tax brought in £68 billion. In 2005-06, it is projected to bring in:

> £138 billion

The projected total tax receipts for 2005-06 are:

> £487 billion   or   £1.3 billion a day

More people are now falling into the higher tax bracket. This is because while wages have gone up, personal allowances and rates have largely stayed put.

Britons are paying the equivalent of 16.5p in the pound on the basic rate of income tax to finance the surge in government spending. If all the new stealth taxes were translated into income tax, the basic rate would rocket from 22p in the pound to 38.5p, which would mean the person earning £25,000 a year would have to pay an extra £60 a week in tax, while anyone on a salary of £40,000 would be almost £100 a week worse off.

And just as it is spending more, the Government is also borrowing more. We obviously pay for this too, even if the Chancellor tries to hide it in PFI deals and the like.

The UK now has a share of indirect taxation significantly above the EU average.

So what are the stealth taxes that have been doing this to us? Below, is a history of tax-creep in the period 1997-2004.

Tax increases since 1997

July 1997

Mortgage tax relief cut; pensions taxed; health insurance tax; health tax raised again; fuel tax escalator raised; vehicle excise duty up; tobacco duty escalator raised; stamp duty on properties over £250,000; corporation tax changed; windfall tax on utilities.

A bad year for – *young people, old people, ill people, drivers, smokers, driving smokers, people in the South, property buyers and sellers.*

March 1998

Married couple's allowance cut; travel insurance tax raised; tax on casinos and fruit machines raised; fuel tax escalator brought forward; car tax upped; foreign earnings tax relief abolished; professions tax concessions abolished; capital gains tax imposed on non-residents; new restrictions on CGT relief; corporation tax payments brought forward; higher stamp duty rates raised; some hydrocarbon duties up; extra diesel duty; landfill tax raised.

A bad year for – *married people, explorers, gamblers, drivers, car owners, ex pats, professionals, aliens, businesses, gas guzzlers and binmen.*

March 1999

National insurance contributions earnings limit raised; NICs for the self-employed raised; married couple's allowance abolished; mortgage tax relief abolished; self-employed contractors taxed more; company car mileage allowance limited; tobacco duty escalator brought forward; insurance premium tax up; vocational training tax relief scrapped; employer NICs put on benefits; VAT on some banking services raised; premiums paid to tenants by landlords taxed; duty on domestic fuel oil up; excise duty for lorries raised; landfill tax escalator introduced; top rates of stamp duty raised again.

A bad year for – *taxpayers, self-employed, married couples, house buyers, City folk, Cubans, the accident-prone, the unskilled, bankers, landlords, drivers, truckers and dumpers.*

March 2000

Tobacco duty up; top rates of stamp duty up again; extra tax on life assurance companies; tax haven rules tightened.

A bad year for – *foreign wealthy wizards with a death wish.*

April 2002

Personal allowance frozen; NI threshold frozen; NICs for employees up; NICs for employers up; NICs for self-employed up; North Sea tax up; tax on some alcoholic drinks up; new stamp duty regime; corporate debt rules tightened.

A bad year for – *individuals, groups, groups of individuals, employees, employers, the employable, oil drillers, and drinkers.*

April 2003

VAT on electronically supplied services; domestic staff brought into national insurance regime; betting duty changed; tax on red diesel and fuel oil up; tax haven rules change to cover Irish offshoots; vehicle excise duty up.

A **bad year for** – *dot coms, au pairs, whippet fanciers, boat trippers, potato investors and getaway drivers.*

March 2004

Small business tax; white vans taxed; transfer pricing tax raised; increase on taxes for trusts; duty on red diesel raised again; Liquified petroleum gas tax up.

A **bad year for** – *corner shops, Essex man, orphans, tractor drivers, captains of industry and captains of supertankers.*

Every April

Council tax raised.

A **bad year for** – *everyone.*

It wasn't always like this. If you go further back in time and look at the figures for government expenditure as a percentage of GDP, you can see how the state has become ever greedier in confiscating money from its citizens.

The chart opposite, which comes from the House of Commons Library, tells the story. It shows the relentless increase in state

Taxes over time

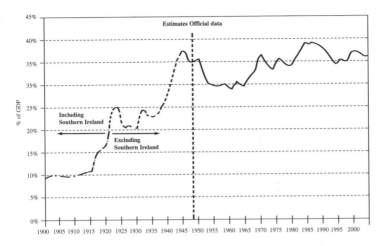

spending over the 20th Century. From 1900-1916 the state contented itself with about 10 per cent of GDP. Then came the First World War, followed by the Great Depression and, after that, the Second World War. With each of these crises, the state ratcheted up public spending to buy anti-Zeppelin bullets, soup kitchens and HMS Hood. Which, obviously, meant more taxes.

From 1945 there was a slow drop for a decade and a half, but this only took us back half way to the pre-WW2 era, and the downwards trend was soon reversed.

The third phase from 1960 to the present shows a general upward trend, punctuated by occasional blips downward.

This historical perspective puts the modern position into

context. We are so conditioned into thinking that the state has a right to a massive share of our earnings that questioning even a couple of per cent of it is almost a modern heresy. Intriguingly, even the full force of the Thatcherite Revolution in the early 80s barely took the tax take from the economy down to the levels of the Attlee Government! So big is the behemoth of government.

Let's zoom in to the top right-hand corner of the diagram. Remember, this is looking at the rate above 30 per cent of GDP, so there is an iceberg of tax below the chart.

Recent Net Taxes and Social Security Contributions as a percentage of total national turnover

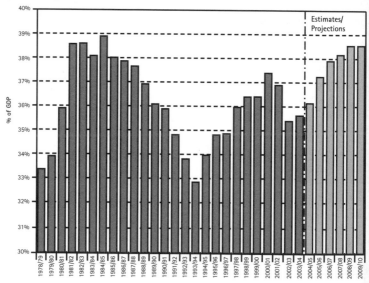

The chart underlines what's been happening to our personal taxes. They were lower in the 70s (unless you ran a business or were fabulously wealthy, in which case you were squeezed "until the pips squeaked"). Then they increased in the early 80s with the Recession, before dropping steadily. At the same time falls in business taxes were taking place, so the overall tax rate dropped.

This trend was reversed under John Major in the mid 90s, in part due to the economic policy disaster behind Black Wednesday, but also due to a return to a social spending tendency by a more left-leaning (though supposedly Conservative) government.

The key pointer as to where we are heading is that the UK economy is not now in recession, yet under New Labour the tendency to tax is increasing regardless. Just look at the projections from 2005-2010. It has to tax, to cover for the large amounts of money being thrown at the public sector.

There is another point to be made. If the Government is borrowing money as well as increasing taxes, who is it borrowing from? Answer – the international banking community. This means that it's not even UK citizens who are getting the benefit of the Government's recklessness, unlike our past history during our continental wars. UK taxpayers are paying foreign banks.

A record 23 per cent of gilts are owned by overseas investors, which means a national foreign debt of £88 billion. Because our Government has been borrowing so much, it is finding it increasingly hard to find lenders. So notwithstanding all the promises of investment, the prospect of the Government actually being forced into cost cutting is very real over the medium term. Whether they will be sensible cuts is a different matter.

What does this mean? Simply put:

---

1. The Government is living beyond its means.

2. It is being shortsighted by borrowing. Loans will have to be repaid later, with interest.

3. Even stealth taxes hurt.

4. The trend is getting worse, not better.

5. Cutting taxes in a way that's 'radical' to some politicians today, would in reality only be taking us back to the days of Callaghan or Heath!

The International Context

Independent economists from around the world increasingly agree that gross inefficiency is endemic in Britain's public sector. Even the Government's own statisticians have expressed disquiet.

The most rigorous assessment of the size and scope of the problem comes in a July 2003 working paper from the European Central Bank called *'Public sector efficiency: an international comparison'.*

To assess the efficiency of state sectors across countries in the Organisation for Economic Co-operation and Development (OECD), the authors, Antonio Afonso and Ludger Schuknecht from the ECB, and Vito Tanzi who works for the Italian government, took into account the size of public spending as well as a series of socio-economic indicators as proxies for performance. What they discovered is truly shocking:

If Britain's public spending were as efficient as that of the US, or Japan, the British government could spend 16 per cent less than it currently does, while still producing the same level of public services.

The authors assess that a level of public spending somewhere between 30 and 35 per cent of GDP "was likely to provide the government of a country with resources sufficient to support all the activities that genuinely merit public support".

The savings entailed would allow for a dramatic downsizing of government and huge tax cuts, boosting the sustainable rate of economic growth, and hence jobs and prosperity.

Given that government spending is expected to have reached over £518 billion in the current 2005-06 fiscal year, this suggests that public spending and hence taxes could be slashed by about £83 billion without any deterioration in service quality – an estimate just above the £82 billion reached in this book.

In stark contrast to the gross inefficiency of the British public sector, overall efficiency is highest in Japan, Luxembourg, Australia, the US and Switzerland. But the most important fact to emerge from the ECB research is that countries with relatively small state sectors do significantly better than countries with medium-sized or big ones. Size, as they say, isn't everything.

That's not the only intriguing conclusion the ECB stat gurus have come up with. In a 2005 paper snappily called *'Reforming Public Expenditure in Industrialized Countries: Are There Trade-offs?'* they found that all the evidence denounced the old, big tax shibboleths.

- Contrary to common beliefs, over the past two decades several countries have been able to reduce public spending by remarkable amounts. These countries did not seem to suffer from the large reductions either financially or socially. On the contrary, ambitious expenditure reform coincided with improvements in fiscal, economic, human development and institutional indicators.

- Case studies of the really ambitious reformers support the view that there is life after public spending reductions. These countries have been among the best economic performers in recent years. The fear that cuts in spending bring economic slowdown has not materialised.

- The UK reformed in many areas. But early progress with public expenditure reduction was, to a significant extent, reversed in later years.

- In several cases, reform efforts often just reversed earlier government expansion. Public spending in the groups of late reformers in 2002, for example, was little changed from twenty years earlier (despite the recent reform efforts) and it was much higher than in the countries that reformed early.

- A country that wants to reduce its public expenditure ratio by a significant size has to tackle welfare programmes. Other expenditure categories offer fewer opportunities for reduction. Over the long run a reduction in public debt can also make a major contribution to the reduction in public spending when the initial debt level is high.

- Studies have pointed to underlying reasons why social spending is poorly targeted: public investment is not always productive; and government consumption does not necessarily mean more education or more security but at times more waste and red tape. Higher taxes and less innovation and productivity may actually translate into less employment and wage gains for lower income individuals.

- Stronger growth has on average moderated, and in some cases over-compensated for, the changes in the income share of the poorest fifth of the population for the countries which were ambitious reformers. For example, since 1990, the absolute position of the poorest fifth has improved most among ambitious and early reformers (from 5 per cent below average to 5 per cent above). At the same time, the position of the poor in timid and late reformers may not have deteriorated much within the country but it has relative to those that grew faster.

So, to summarise, if you really shake up your welfare state, you can cut taxes, which makes people richer. Even the poorest people in society get better off as a result.

But if you do nothing, you are doing nobody any favours.

Unfortunately, Gordon Brown is moving Britain away from its traditionally relatively small state sector model. Instead, we are moving towards the big-government model found in countries such as socialist Sweden, which could slash spending by 43 per cent if it achieved US-style efficiency, according to the ECB report.

The UK will undoubtedly tumble further down the state-sector efficiency league table in years to come, as more and more of the billions the Chancellor is pouring into the state sector are wasted.

Robert Mugabe
President of Zimbabwe
c/o Embassy of the Republic of
Zimbabwe
429 The Strand
London
WC2R 0JR

December 2005

Dear Mr. Mugabe,

It has been reported in the British media that you are chauffeured in a Mercedes S600L Pullman limousine, which comes fully equipped with a CD player, movies and Internet access. It has also been suggested that your 21-foot, 5-tonne vehicle, powered by a V12 dual turbo engine, can only do 11 miles per gallon.

We are currently compiling a Bumper Book of Government Waste and we were wondering whether you would be willing to send us a photograph of your limousine along with a short statement commenting on whether it constitutes either "government waste" or "extravagance". We would also be interested to hear your views on global warming.

Thank you in anticipation of your help.

Yours sincerely,

Matthew Elliott
TPA Chief Executive

"There is no art which one government sooner learns from another than that of draining money from the pockets of its people."

Adam Smith

Waste Watchdogs

A variety of public and private watchdogs produce estimates of government waste. In this section, we look at those estimates, and, implicitly, at the potential savings to be made from cutting back on unnecessary, and poorly executed spending.

Let's start with one type of spending that everybody agrees is wasteful – fraud.

Fraud

Public Accounts Committee	£11 billion
Centre for Retail Research	£18.5 billion

The wide margin between the two figures is explained by the fact that the PAC calculated identified fraud only, while the CRR was an estimate of identified *and* unidentified fraud.

Government Waste

Both the Government and the Conservatives have recognised that on top of fraud, the system itself is inherently wasteful. And both of them carried out studies before the last general election to examine the specifics.

Sir Peter Gershon was asked by the Treasury to look at the problem from an insider's perspective. Critics point out that, given who commissioned the report, he was hardly likely to conclude that the vast amounts injected into the system by the Government have been wasted. Therefore, his conclusions can be assumed to be somewhat restrained.

Notwithstanding this, the *Gershon Review* has at least introduced government departments to a concept they have never encountered before: the idea of making cutbacks and efficiency savings. Private sector companies do it all the time; why not the public sector? The reforms being considered include relocating staff outside London, and reducing civil service numbers. They are taking rather long to implement, but at least there is some movement.

The Conservatives, for their part, turned to the Millenium Dome troubleshooter David James and his team to come up with an independent set of figures. The 173-page *James Report* has also come under criticism for identifying many of the problems without being bold enough to recommend wiping them out. One example is the surge in spending on outside consultancy, where, having noted that spending was up by 600 per cent, James only recommended that it be cut by a third.

The *Gershon* and *James* recommendations which we quote below were, therefore, politically-driven calculations of what level of government waste was 'politically acceptable' for each of the major parties in the run-up to the last election.*

Gershon Review/Labour	£21.5 billion
James Report/Conservative	£35 billion

---

* If you have any doubt about this, remember what happened to Howard Flight, the Conservative Treasury spokesman, when his private view that more waste savings might be found once the Conservatives were in office was made public. Michael Howard withdrew the whip and prevented him from standing for election.

On top of these, you can add the estimate provided by Edward Leigh MP, the Chairman of the House of Commons Public Accounts Committee. He believes that the amount of waste is higher than the *James Report*, but cautiously limits his ceiling in the absence of official statistics.

Public Accounts Committee Chairman   £58 billion

Two studies have actually gone into the combined details of fraud and government waste. The European Central Bank has, on more than one occasion, undertaken comparative studies on optimal taxation and state spending, and by applying its analysis of where the Laffer curve lies with Western European state models, it is clear that the real level of waste is far higher than either *Gershon* or *James* admit.

The TaxPayers' Alliance, for our part, reached the same ball park figure by an entirely separate route. Our bottom-up approach was to isolate the various examples of identifiable waste and then add them together. Anoraks with time on their hands can check out our breakdown at the end of this chapter.

So the following estimates are of actual waste.

TaxPayers' Alliance   £82 billion
European Central Bank   £83 billion

We believe that cutting back on anything less than £82 billion is leaving large amounts of money going straight down the drain.

How is the Government doing? To judge by the December 2005 report overleaf, not very well.

Public Accounts Committee

"Despite signs of progress, however, in too many areas we have seen too little progress over the last decade. In particular, the Committee continues to see cases of:

- policies not being properly planned or thought through;

- improvements not materialising or taking place slowly, despite promises;

- failure to apply more widely the lessons learned in one part of the public sector;

- the repetition of mistakes, even after the causes have been identified;

- failure to exploit commercial opportunities; and

- slow progress in making the most of opportunities offered by new developments in technology.

For many years, the Committee of Public Accounts, through its scrutiny of departments' use of public funds, has consistently highlighted practical ways to achieve better value for money for the taxpayer. The Committee has also emphasised the need for careful planning in order to increase the chance of successful implementation of policies, and urged government to act on the evidence in our reports that departments lack well developed capabilities in a range of skills. Many of our recommendations have not required radical change; indeed they are often about basic housekeeping and good management."

PAC *'Achieving Value for Money in the Delivery of Public Services'* Dec 2005

The TPA's £82 billion

So, where does the TPA's £82 billion estimate of waste come from? Below are the most significant examples of wasteful spending from *The Bumper Book*, adding up to just over £82 billion. Remember, this is below the ECB's estimate of £83 billion, so we're not alone in thinking that this much money is wasted.

Figure	Item	Page #
£20m	Savings from halving £40m cost of NHS staff suspensions	44
£30m	NHS computer training for cleaners and porters	46
£83m	Public sector fraud and overpayments	127
£100m	NHS Ghost Patients	43
£100m	Teachers who never teach	58
£109m	Cutting the cost of MEPs to £1m each	152
£110m	Common Fisheries Policy	67
£117m	Bogus or excessive compensation claims against councils	104
£120m	Overly-sophisticated police digital radio system	26
£130m	Overspend on legal aid budget	19
£144m	Extra spending on Govt. advertising since 1997	70
£200m	Health tourism	42
£200m	Waste in public libraries	104

£208m	**Selling government assets** - The Royal Mint and Bisham Abbey would provide a windfall of £208m	128
£214m	Unused repeat prescriptions	44
£257m	New Deal for Communities	103
£300m	Supporting failed asylum seekers	29
£329m	EU fraud and mismanagement	145
£375m	E-Government websites that do not resolve customer queries	110
£450m	MOD's £600m compensation bill has quadrupled over the past ten years	91
£575m	Missed NHS appointments	76
£677m	Cost of New Deal	42
£1bn	**Illnesses caught in NHS hospitals** - According to the NAO, hospital-acquired infections cost the NHS as much as £1 billion per year.	40
£1bn	**Bird-killing wind farms** - The Government's £1 billion a year spending programme on wind farms has been condemned by conservationists such as David Bellamy for killing rare birds.	66
£1.08bn	**State sector absenteeism** - State employees take 10.7 days off "sick" a year, compared to 7.8 in the private sector. The total cost of state sector sickness is £4 billion so the extra time taken off costs taxpayers £1.08 billion. The worst offenders are the prison service (£80m cost) and the DWP (£100m).	131
£1.1bn	**Overpayment of benefits** - Over £1.1 billion is	

owed to the Department for Work and Pensions from benefit recipients who have been overpaid.   78

£1.2bn   **The growing cost of government regulation** - The Government spends over £12 billion a year regulating our lives and businesses. If all government regulators tightened their belts by 10 per cent – as private firms regularly do – taxpayers could save £1.2 billion.   61

£1.24bn   **Public sector IT projects** - According to the Work and Pensions Committee, public sector IT expenditure is in excess of £12.4 billion, "with a significant proportion at risk of being wasted". Assuming just 10 per cent is wasteful means potential savings of £1.24 billion.   109

£1.93bn   **British subsidy to overseas farmers** - Britain's net contribution to the EU budget is currently £4.3 billion a year. About 45 per cent of the budget is allocated to the Common Agricultural Policy, which means that £1.93 billion of British taxpayers' money went to overseas farmers.   66

£2.38bn   **Overspend on NHS IT** - The NHS National Programme for IT (NPfIT) will cost up to five times the previously stated cost of £6.2 billion over 10 years, meaning that the total bill could be as high as £30 billion, representing an overspend of £2.38 billion a year for ten years.   111

£2.5bn   **Network Rail's inefficiency** - In December 2003, the Rail Regulator said that more than £1,000 million of Network Rail's annual spending was work "that the company does not need to do" and that £1.5 billion could be saved "by eliminating waste and inefficiency".   55

£2.6bn	**Fraud and error in the benefits system** - According to a 2005 NAO report, fraud and mistakes in the benefits system cost taxpayers £2.6 billion a year. Labour MP Frank Field believes that the real figure could be as high as £7 billion.	77
£2.68bn	**Unfair Barnett Formula** - If state spending per person living in Scotland was reduced to the level of spending per person in the north of England, taxpayers would save £2.68 billion a year.	99
£2.7bn	**Overspending on defence procurement** - According to the National Audit Office, the cost of major defence projects went over budget by £2.7 billion last year, not to mention major delivery delays.	90
£2.94bn	**NHS compensation claims** - Clinical negligence claims cost at least £5.89 billion and could be as high as £9 billion. Saving half of the lower figure would save taxpayers £2.94 billion.	41
£3bn	**Inefficient local government procurement** - According to the Confederation of British Industry, councils are wasting at least £3 billion a year because they are not squeezing value for money out of contractors.	105
£4bn	**Unnecessary incapacity benefit** - A Government minister admitted that a third of the country's 2.7 million Incapacity Benefit claimants could work immediately. This would save taxpayers £4 billion of the total £12 billion cost.	79
£4.1bn	**Smaller examples of government waste** - Five per cent of our total represents all the smaller examples of government waste detailed in *The Bumper Book*.	-

| £5bn | **Abolishing the DTI** - The Liberal Democrats recognise that the Department for Trade and Industry is a waste of money and are calling for its abolition, saving taxpayers £5 billion. | 62 |

£5.54bn **Central government administration** - The Government is spending £21.3 billion on administration in 2005/6, an increase of over 40% since 1998/99. During that time, prices have gone up by roughly 14%. This 26-point difference represents £5.54 billion of inefficiency and inflation-busting pay rises for the public sector. 131

£6bn **NHS inefficiency** - An Office for National Statistics report in 2004 suggested that the NHS was wasting up to £6 billion a year due to rising inefficiency. Since then, spending has increased and productivity has declined even further so this is a conservative estimate. 38

£7bn **Equal employment conditions** - Equalising the retirement age and pension provision for public sector workers so that they are in line with the private sector would save an estimated £7 billion. 138

£7.1bn **Balanced budgets** - Government departments overspent their budgets for 2004/5 by £7.1 billion. Prudent financial management by ministers would give taxpayers better value for money. 128

£11.37bn **Axing half of quangos** - Quangoland costs at least £22.7 billion a year. John Reid promised to halve the number of NHS quangos to save £500 million. If the same principle were applied to all quangos, taxpayers would save £11.37 billion. 127

£82.4 billion of waste

A billion here, a billion there

"The packaging of the original Rubik's Cube stated that there were more than three billion states the cube could attain. In fact, there were 4 x (10 to the power of 19) possible states. That is, 4 with 19 zeroes after it.

What the packaging said wasn't wrong; there were more than three billion possible states. The understatement, however, is symptomatic of a pervasive innumeracy which ill suits a technologically based society. It's analagous to the Lincoln Tunnel stating: New York, population more than 6; or McDonald's proudly announcing that they've sold more than 120 hamburgers."

John Allen Paulos, *Innumeracy*

£82,000,000,000

A Big, Bad Number

Bad

£82 billion of waste. Certainly a big number. But a bad one? Yes. There are several different 'costs' from having so much waste in the system.

- Firstly, there is the economic cost. Some of the £82 billion comes from Corporation Tax levied on businesses. Instead of being wasted by government, that money could be used by business to increase competitiveness, invest in new products, undertake R&D and train staff, creating wealth in the process. Siphoning the money off, and then wasting it, is bad for the economy.

- Secondly, the £82 billion of waste hits personal finances. If money is taken out of your pocket and put to inefficient use, you might as well have spent it yourself and kept the admin costs. Everyone is poorer for bad use of public money.

- Thirdly, the more waste there is in the system, the harder it becomes to correct the faults, because the culture of the public sector is self-reinforcing and resists change. No doubt, there are cases where outside consultants need to be brought in because they have the specialist skills to help civil servants. But excessive use of consultants is expensive and helps create a blinkered approach to government, with the advisers tempted into writing only what their paymasters want them to see.

- Fourthly, waste means that the people who need the help most aren't getting it.

- Finally, and most perniciously, what comes out of a blind and wasteful benefits system is a culture of dependency, where people think that the state owes them something in exchange for nothing. The bigger the sink culture becomes, the harder it is to reinvigorate the economy as the vested interest becomes larger. In many ways, that's what brought two centuries of crisis to the world of ancient Rome.

These days, we can laugh at the *Yeah But No But* way of living, but at some point in the not too distant future, the bills will become so painful, it won't be funny. Even Labour Ministers admit that two thirds of incapacity claimants are actually fit to go back to work. Despite better healthcare and fewer industrial injuries, there are four times more people on incapacity benefit than there were 30 years ago. Doctors find it easier to sign sick notes than handle a torrent of abuse. The system has to change, and radically.

Big

Eighty-two billion is a very big number. It's an unfathomably, awesomely, distantly big number.

Not quite as big as the 100 billion stars said to be in our galaxy but, hey, getting there.

Time to put a maths O-Level to use . . .

- £82 billion would buy, at retail rates, a Scooby Doo DVD for absolutely everyone on the planet, and there would still be £2 billion in change – enough to control malaria worldwide.

- A £5 note is roughly 13cm long and 7cm wide. If you laid out 82 billion five pound notes end to end, the line would stretch 2,366,000 km, or 37 times round the earth. That's even more than Tony Blair travels in a year. It's three times to the moon and back.

- It would take 846,154 fivers to cover an international sized football pitch. That means that £82,000,000,000 worth would cover one to the depth of around 2.15 metres. That's a pile over seven feet high. Liverpool's Peter Crouch, at 6'7", would still be five inches out of sight.

Never mind the trivia. More sobering is the thought of what £82 billion could have done for this country. It could have written off the national debt over five years (or at least, what the Government admits to owing), which could have saved us the £22 billion that we're paying as a nation in interest every year.

Or it could have gone towards funding £82 billion of tax cuts.

That's enough to:

-   Return over £4,000 to each British household, a sum that would pay every family's entire transport budget or total food and clothing expenditure.

-   Abolish National Insurance contributions (£82.6 billion).

In addition, because the huge tax cuts identified would boost employment, spending and economic growth, they would also lead in turn to additional revenues for the Exchequer from VAT and income tax – which means that taxes could be cut even more than suggested in this book, without increasing the budget deficit.

Furthermore, compliance costs, including legal and accounting fees, would be saved and a huge amount of time freed up for more productive pursuits. Large sections of the Inland Revenue could be scrapped, generating significant additional savings.

Inheritance tax has understandably become Britain's most hated and resented tax. It now even hits people who bought their own council homes in the 1980s, and most of the revenues it raises seem to do little more than keep bureaucrats comfortable. It's a legitimate target.

The abolition of NICs and inheritance tax or huge cuts to income tax would transform British competitiveness, creating hundreds of thousands of jobs as global businesses would choose to relocate to Britain.

And having not forked out all this tax, you could have kept it.

Let's put the sums involved into an imaginable context.

Say you, as an individual, got £1,400 back in the post from the taxman tomorrow and every year. This is the comparative value of that amount of money. You could have bought:

- A holiday in the Maldives followed by a holiday in St Kitts

- Three months in Butlins in Bognor Regis

- A flight to Australia, a surfboard and 400 cans of Fosters

- A new washing machine, cooker and tumble dryer, and a French maid to come in for an hour once a week to service them

- A second-hand hang glider

- A new bed, sofa and armchair

- A plasma TV

- Five years' private health care cover for a 50-year-old

Or, if you are 21, you could invest it every year in a pensions package that would mature into a pot of a quarter of a million by the time you retire.

"The government is like a baby's alimentary canal, with a happy appetite at one end and no responsibility at the other."

Ronald Reagan

The Case for Lower Taxes

Taxes transfer resources from the private sector, which is relatively efficient, to the state sector, which, as we have seen, is extremely inefficient. Higher taxes increase the share of national output handed over to the state, which reduces the economy's overall efficiency. Because productivity growth in the state sector is far lower than in the private sector, hiring more state workers invariably reduces the efficiency of the economy as a whole. And lower overall productivity growth means lower economic growth.

With higher inflation in the state sector than in the private sector, taxpayers obtain far less value for their money when it is spent on their behalf by government officials than when they are allowed to spend it themselves. This too leads to reduced economic growth. A hypothetical 10 per cent increase in spending on private goods and services would boost output by more than 8.6 per cent; the same 10 per cent increase in spending on the state sector will translate into output growth of under 8 per cent.

Taxes also reduce the incentive for private companies and individuals to work, save, invest, take risks and start new businesses, reducing economic growth. The disincentive is particularly marked among entrepreneurs, older workers, part-time workers and second-earners in two-income families. When taxes become oppressive, these sort of people work less hard and may even withdraw from the labour market altogether. Cutting marginal tax rates on income and profits would boost economic growth by improving incentives.

A study from the OECD found that every 1 percentage point increase in taxes as a share of GDP reduces per capita output levels by between 0.3 per cent and 0.6 per cent. And a further report by PricewaterhouseCoopers found that every 1 percentage point of GDP increase in distortionary taxation reduces economic growth by between 0.2 and 0.4 points a year.

The chart below shows the massive extra growth that would be achieved over the next five years using PwC's findings and our proposed £82 billion tax cuts.

**GDP growth over next 5 years –
Impact of lower taxes (£k per household)**

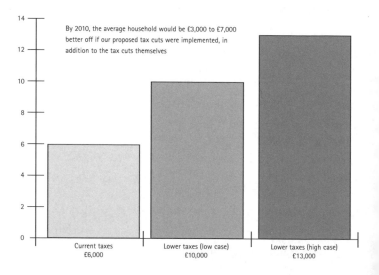

By 2010, the average household would be £3,000 to £7,000 better off if our proposed tax cuts were implemented, in addition to the tax cuts themselves

| Current taxes £6,000 | Lower taxes (low case) £10,000 | Lower taxes (high case) £13,000 |

By 2010, the average household would be £2,000 to £4,500 better off if our proposed tax cuts were implemented, in addition to the tax cuts themselves. But despite the evidence, Gordon Brown still believes he can tax us to prosperity – an attitude which is inflicting irreparable damage on the British economy.

There are also very strong moral and ethical reasons why taxes should be cut. The contemporary debate in British politics is based on the flawed premise that the government is entitled to decide how the wealth and income created by the people of this country can be spent. This is best exemplified by a slightly sinister phrase, which is often read in newspapers or heard on television: the claim that tax cuts are a 'cost to the government'.

We couldn't disagree more. Tax revenues belong to those who earned the money in the first place, not to the government, politicians or 'society'. At the heart of the TaxPayers' Alliance's ethical case for lower taxes is a belief in the sanctity of private property rights. Individuals have a natural right to their property, including their income.

Taxes are a violation of those private property rights and should therefore be minimised. Some taxes are unavoidable. However, it should never be forgotten that they are at best a necessary evil.

The only truly moral way for people to interact with each other is through mutual consent, with each individual respecting the equal rights of others. Trade, gifts and bequests are all voluntary and are therefore highly moral activities. Taxation, by contrast, is based on force, rather than consent: taxpayers do not voluntarily relinquish a huge chunk of their income to the Exchequer every year. If they did, taxes would not be compulsory.

We firmly believe that the campaign for lower taxes has the moral high ground; it is those who believe in ever higher taxes who should ask themselves whether their ethical principles are not in fact highly questionable.

Britain's tax system is also morally defective because it punishes the most productive citizens; those who already contribute the most. With 'progressive' taxes, the more goods and services an individual or a company are able to produce, the more tax they have to pay.

Wealth and income are also often taxed twice, which is another clear breach of natural justice. For example, profits are taxed when generated by a company, and then again when they are paid out as dividends.

We are now in the 21st Century; it is time to put the collectivist ideologies that ravaged the 20th Century well and truly behind us, and to recognise that a low tax society is also a good society.

The welfare state and NHS are nearly 60 years old. Imagine if your family had lived in the same house for 60 years and how much stuff you could accumulate. Cupboards full, boxes piled high, junk everywhere. But what if every time you tried to throw anything away, one member of the family said, "No, stop. I need that!" You would start to feel like there was no room left to live in. This is how taxpayers feel nowadays. The state crowds them out so that there is little space left to live in. It is time for a clear out, and this report shows us where to start.

Time is short. While we are frittering our taxes on bureaucracy, we are facing a supercrisis in the shape of a pensions meltdown. Our liabilities currently triple the national debt. Every year we delay taking radical action makes the final medicine tougher to swallow. We need determined leadership and bold decisions today, in order to avoid having to make cruel decisions in twenty years' time.

The Axioms Revisited

Back on page 14, we introduced the *Taxpayers' Axioms*. What do you suppose would have happened if the simple job of compiling those axioms had fallen to a government department?

Well, you can be pretty sure that they would have taken five times as long to compile, because as we know, Whitehall likes to operate at its own, unhurried pace.

Then there's the budget. Sky high, of course, and rocketing completely out of control. Most of the money would be blown on focus groups, diversity advisers, best practice champions, and general paper-shufflers. Only a fraction would be reserved for the writer.

When, after several months, a first draft did emerge, it would accidentally be wiped out by a bug in the computer system, and the process would have to start anew. No one would take the blame.

There would never be twelve axioms. Oh, they'd be *written*, but absenteeism being so integral to the public sector ethos, several axioms would pull a sickie on print day.

A huge multi-million pound marketing campaign would be launched to market the axioms, then relaunched for extra PR effect a year later. The Government would pronounce it a huge success.

The whole farce would be paid for by you and me.

Conclusion

Over the course of this book, we've taken you through the fantasy world of public sector spending. We've seen a range of man-made disasters, lunatic schemes, wishful thinking, dopey planning and plain greed.

And yet we've only skimmed the surface.

We've scarcely mentioned the spin doctors, but then they 'only' cost a few million every year. This includes the £300,000 said to be the going rate for the three people hired to take over from Alastair Campbell.

Then there are the Special Advisers, the policy wonks brought into the ministers' offices to play the politics that civil servants aren't supposed to. Their numbers have now doubled to 80. In 2004, they cost the taxpayer £360,000 in foreign trips, to add to their £5.3 million salaries. That averages out at about £65,000 each, several thousand more than an MP gets. They are also eligible for three months' severance pay, an expression that sadly promises more than it delivers.

You could further add the £400,000 spent on hiring consultants to monitor the negative media reporting of five departments. What is clear is that the Government has become a consultancy junkie. The Department of Health has symptomatically spent £608,000 on ten different firms of consultants solely to implement the cost cutting expected after the *Gershon Review*.

In 2004, spending on consultants had gone up by nearly half. It had risen to £1.86 billion – but that's an underestimate as it only counts the trade association that covers two in three consultants, so the real total is probably approaching £3 billion. The average outsider brought in costs ten times the rate of a comparable civil servant. Even then, they are frequently too close to government to be valuable as independent consultants. One consultancy provides half the advisers of the independent regulator of Foundation Hospitals. Another wrote, in advance of the 2005 election, a surprisingly neutral report on City Academies. Ironically, Lord Birt, adviser to Blair, has been forced to retire as a consultant to the consultants whom his boss was consulting.

What is particularly ludicrous is that, contrary to the Government's own rules, there are reports of former civil servants who had been made redundant being hired back as consultants to do the same job at an increased rate of pay.

We've also noticed in the course of researching this book how the Government spends your money advertising itself. The advertising bill now comes to over £200 million a year, which is three times higher than it was ten years ago.

There are also fault lines within the civil service itself. Some are due to duff units being set up for politically correct ends, like the £90 million allocated to the new 'Respect' unit, or the £19 million direct costs estimate for "coordinating strategy across gender, race, disability and civil service work force representation".

Our research has revealed that, despite privatisation, the state still owns a lot of assets. We're not saying that they should all be sold. It is right that items of special historical interest and value should be preserved for the nation, ideally in a manner that either makes them accessible to the public, or projects national prestige to foreign dignitaries, and preferably both.

We do, however, take note of the hypocrisy of some New Labour figures who pontificated from a lofty height about the disgrace of a Royal Yacht being bought for the Sovereign to host trade events on; and who then find themselves revelling in surroundings of imperial swank when they themselves get to the top.

For instance, the Cabinet Office has a set of five carved gilt wood armchairs worth half a million; a carved gilt wood furniture suite worth another half a million; a Harewood commode worth £350,000; a white marble bust of Oliver Cromwell worth £350,000; and an antique wooden table known as the 'Treasury Table' worth a quarter of a million.

Despite having these and other similar assets at its disposal, the Whitehall arts budget still dispenses £500,000 every year for decorating Whitehall buildings with paintings borrowed from museums.

Incidentally, 10/11 Downing Street is valued at £23,625,942. That random detail might win you some money in a pub quiz some day.

Another aspect of government waste we've barely touched on is overseas travel. When Blair went off on his 2005 Caribbean cruise, did he really have to hire two extra 46ft catamarans for his security team? They set the taxpayer back around £10,000.

We've also uncovered the fact that the Culture Secretary and her staff flew out to New York to attend the London Symphony Orchestra Centenary Gala. With accommodation, that cost £7,740.

Then there was the Leader of the Commons' six day visit with staff to Australia and New Zealand "to take forward work in the modernisation of the House of Commons and facilitate business links with the Welsh Development Agency". Yeah, right. Cost – £9,839. This is the same Geoff Hoon, incidentally, who in April 2003 annoyed the troops waiting overnight in Basrah for transport home, when he flew back after a visit and was reported locally to have had spaces on the plane.

We calculate that in the year to March 2005, Blair's own travel cost the taxpayer nearly £800,000. It was, though, an election year. The two previous years came to around £930,000. For 2001-02, he and his team chalked up a whopping £1.7 million bill.

The Leader of Lords was positively frugal by comparison. In 2002, he cost the public purse £4,000 attending a meeting of the Bilderberg Group, the secretive gathering of world movers and shakers so beloved of conspiracy theorists.

The list goes on and on. There's the National Auditors' report which says that part of the £510 million budget dedicated to dealing with the 1.4 million complaints received every year could be saved simply by removing the confusion that gives rise to the complaints in the first place.

And there's the urgent need to clarify policy regarding disabilities. An official New Labour strategy report came to the bewildering conclusion that eleven million people in the UK, or one in four of the adult population, are disabled. This compares with three million who are on benefits. Such politics of apologetics do no one any favours. Money has been thrown at a group which is clearly deserving, but whose militant campaigners too often make demands that carry extortionate costs.

If pedestrian footbridges over railways cost ten times as much to install if they are to be disabled-friendly, then the result now seems to be that they don't get built at all. Tax money is also squandered without any clear purpose or direction as a blindfolded response to this problem. £370 million has been budgeted by the Department of Transport over ten years to provide accessibility improvements – but a third of this sum is earmarked for disability awareness training.

And of course there are the massive pensions liabilities this country is storing up for itself. Just one man, the Head of the Civil Service, has a pension with a transferable value estimated at a shade under two million pounds.

The bill for all this is coming straight out of your wallet.

Edward Gibbon tells us in *The Decline and Fall of the Roman Empire* that in ancient times, a Locrian who proposed any new law stood in front of the assembly of the people with a cord round his neck: if the law was accepted, his life was spared; if the law was rejected, the innovator was instantly strangled.

Some of the examples of government waste in this book are a result of cock-ups or good intentions going wrong. However, other cases, such as Lord Irvine's infamous wallpaper, are clear examples of extravagance with our money.

We do not go so far as to propose the Locrian test for new government spending projects. But greater ministerial accountability for wasteful spending is long overdue. It's time to cut money for old rope.

Making a Stand on Waste

Pay as You Earn (PAYE) was introduced by the British government in 1944, when it feared that a temporary blip in payments might damage the war effort. It has been with us ever since. Central government has rarely had to fear the threat of money being withheld in protest at its incompetence.

That threat does exist for local government, which depends upon people coughing up when they are billed. But what if your money is clearly being frittered away and you are living on the breadline?

The martyrs of the battle for fairer and lower taxes are undoubtedly Sylvia Hardy and Reverend Alfred Ridley, two pensioners who went to jail in 2005 in protest at the above-inflation increase in their council tax bills. Many more pensioners have pledged to follow their bold footsteps in 2006 to highlight how council tax is driving taxpayers into poverty.

10p from every copy of *The Bumper Book of Government Waste* sold will be donated to a special fighting fund to support brave tax protesters such as Mrs Hardy and Reverend Ridley.

The fund will be administered by IsItfair, the grassroots council tax protest group that has done so much to highlight the inequity of council tax and the debilitating tax burden on pensioners.

We urge you to support this important battle by signing up to IsItfair through their website www.isitfair.co.uk. And don't forget to also join the TaxPayers' Alliance!

Further Reading

Books

'*The Great Deception*' - Christopher Booker, Richard North - 2005, Continuum

'*The Peter Principle*' - C. Northcote-Parkinson - 1969, Souvenir

'*The Wealth of Nations*' - Adam Smith - 1776, Bantam Classics

Reports

'*A Cost Too Far?*' - Ian Milne - Civitas, 2004

'*Achieving value for money in the delivery of public services*' - Public Accounts Committee - December 2005

'*Britain and Europe: the Balance Sheet*' - Professor Patrick Minford CBE - MCB University Press, 1996, and subsequent

'*Better Off Out?*' - Hindley and Howe - Institute of Economic Affairs 2001, and subsequent

'*Manifesto for Reform*'- Reform - February 2005

'*Public sector efficiency: an international comparison*' - Antonio Afonso, Ludger Schuknecht and Vito Tanzi - European Central Bank working paper 242, 2003

'*Releasing Resources for the Frontline: Independent Review of Public Sector Efficiency*' - Sir Peter Gershon, HM Treasury, 2004

Websites

www.taxpayersalliance.com

4 reasons to support the Taxpayers' Alliance...

1 – Higher taxes hurt ordinary families

Since 1995 politicians have increased taxes for the average family by an astonishing £4,000. That's £4,000 that could have provided a family with a new computer to help with a child's homework, and left enough to pay for a family holiday.

2 – Council Tax rises aren't fair

Council tax bills have increased by 76 per cent since 1997. The average family now pays £1,200 a year in council tax – and bills are set to rise further. Some pensioners have been sent to jail because they cannot afford the outrageous increases.

3 – Politicians waste our taxes

The European Central Bank estimates that politicians waste over £80 billion a year. That's equivalent to the annual running cost of the NHS.

4 – Higher taxes damage the economy

Higher taxes will make Britain a less attractive place to do business – a serious mistake when countries such as India and China are increasingly competitive.

"... if you don't trust politicians, why trust them with so much of your money?"

REGISTER FREE AS A TAXPAYERS' ALLIANCE SUPPORTER

Name: _____

Home Address:_____

_____

Email:_____

Home Telephone Number:_____

Mobile:_____

Occupation: _____

Senior Citizen (tick) ☐

Please send this form back to:

The TaxPayers' Alliance
Box 101
95 Wilton Road
London
SW1V 1BZ

You can also register your support on the campaign website:

www.taxpayersalliance.com

Or you can call 0845 330 9554

Tell a friend about The Bumper Book of Government Waste!

The TaxPayers' Alliance exists to campaign for responsible and accountable taxation. If, having read our book, you agree with what we're trying to do, please spread the word!

One way to do this is to tell a friend about this book. Simply fill out your friend's address on the page opposite, tear it out and send them all the details.

Thanks for your support!

Harriman House Publishing

Harriman House is an independent specialist publisher producing books on business, finance, politics and technology.

For details of all our current and forthcoming publications please go to: www.harriman-house.com

or request a copy of our latest catalogue by sending your details to:

Harriman House Ltd
43 Chapel Street
Petersfield
Hampshire
GU32 3DY

Dear

I have to tell you about this book. It's a must read
and a real eye opener – £82 billion wasted!

The Bumper Book of Government Waste
The scandal of the squandered billions from Lord Irvine's
wallpaper to EU saunas.
by Matthew Elliott and Lee Rotherham
Published by Harriman House
ISBN: 1-897-59779-7
RRP: £9.99

Available direct from the publishers or from all
good bookstores.

www.harriman-house.com

tel 01730 233870

Harriman House Ltd
43 Chapel Street
Petersfield
GU32 3DY

Hh

The
Bumper
Book of
Government Waste

The scandal of the squandered billions from Lord Irvine's wallpaper to EU saunas...

Matthew Elliott & Lee Rotherham